A TREATISE

ON

DIPHTHERIA:

ITS

NATURE, PATHOLOGY,

AND

HOMŒOPATHIC TREATMENT.

BY

WM. TOD HELMUTH, M. D.,

PROFESSOR OF SURGICAL ANATOMY IN THE HOMŒOPATHIC MEDICAL COLLEGE OF MISSOURI; PRESIDENT OF THE ST. LOUIS HOM. MED. SOCIETY; RECORDING SECRETARY OF THE WESTERN INSTITUTE OF HOMŒOPATHY; MEMBER OF THE AMERICAN INSTITUTE OF HOMŒOPATHY; AUTHOR OF SURGERY, AND ITS ADAPTATION TO HOMŒOPATHIC PRACTICE. ETC., ETC.

(*Second Edition, Revised and Corrected.*)

ST. LOUIS HOMŒOPATHIC PHARMACY.

H. C. G. LUYTIES.

MDCCCLXIV.

TO

WILLIAM S. HELMUTH, ESQ., M.D.,

FOR OVER FORTY YEARS AN EARNEST, THOUGH MODEST INVESTIGATOR

OF SCIENTIFIC TRUTH,

WHO FIRST DIRECTED MY STEPS TOWARDS THE PATHS OF MEDICINE,

AND WHO, THROUGH LIFE, HAS GUIDED ME BY EXAMPLE AND ADVICE,

THIS TREATISE IS DEDICATED,

BY HIS NEPHEW,

THE AUTHOR.

PREFACE TO THE FIRST EDITION.

In presenting these pages to the reader, little comment is necessary.

The author has endeavored to incorporate the observation of others with a somewhat extended experience of his own, and thus to produce a readable work upon a disease to which the attention of the whole medical profession has been directed, and which will ever occupy a conspicuous position in the medical history of the nineteenth century.

The substance of the following pages has been prepared, from time to time, at such hours as could be spared from an arduous professional life; a fact, it is hoped, that will, to a certain degree, extenuate the faults and explain the deficiency of the composition.

213 Pine Street,
St. Louis, Mo., April 15th, 1862.

PREFACE TO THE SECOND EDITION.

In offering the Second Edition of this volume to the Profession, the Author would state that he has endeavored to make such alterations and corrections as the present state of our knowledge of Diphtheria demands, and has expunged and modified other portions of the work according to the experience of the best practitioners of the Homœopathic School. A considerable number of pages, treating of the Surgical management of Diphtheria, have been omitted, and their place supplied with other matter which will probably be of more service to the generality of practitioners; enough, however, has been allowed to remain to give the reader an idea of the utility of such means and the opinions of others as to their expediency. The whole chapter on the "*Treatment*," has been re-modeled, and all the newer medicines been added to the list of remedial agents which have been found serviceable in the affection. Sections on the "Manner of Recovery," and "Manner of Death," with some hints as to the further Pathology, have been incorporated with the text.

With such modifications and corrections, the Author would again claim the indulgence of his professional friends, for the many imperfections of this treatise, relying, in a measure, on the favor with which the first edition has been received, and trusting that what has been added will increase the usefulness and practical value of the work.

No. 209 Pine St.,
St. Louis, Mo. Sept. 5th, 1864.

CONTENTS.

CHAPTER I.

DIPHTHERIA.

CHAPTER II.

SYMPTOMS AND DIAGNOSIS.

CHAPTER III.

DIFFERENTIAL DIAGNOSIS.

CHAPTER IV.

CUTANEOUS DIPHTHERIA, CONCOMITANTS.

CHAPTER V.

CHAPTER VI.

PATHOLOGY.

CHAPTER VII.

TREATMENT.

CHAPTER VIII.

SURGICAL OPERATIONS.

DIPHTHERIA.

CHAPTER I.

SECTION I.

Synonyms employed at different eras to designate the disease.

The term Diphtheria is of Greek derivation, the terms Διφθερα and Διφθερις having both the same signification—the prepared skin of an animal. Διφθεριτης and Διφθεριας both signify that which is covered with skin.

The terms that have been used at different periods to designate the disease are—

I. MALUM EGYPTIACUM, as described by Aretæus the Cappadocian, also called by him *Ulcus Syriacus.*

II. MORBUS SUFFOCANS, described by Villa Real, as the disease appeared in Andalusia in 1590–91, the title of the work being "(*Joannis de Villa Real de Signis, Causis, Essentia, Prognostico et Curatione Morbi Suffocantis.*) Compluti 1611."

III. GARROTILLO—described by Fontecha—the title being "(*Disputationes Medicæ super ea quæ Hippocrates, Galenus, Avicenas, necnon et alii Græci,*

Arabes et Latini, de Anginarum naturis, speciebus causis et curationibus scripsere diversis in locis; et circa affectionem hisce temporibus vocatam GARROTILLO. Opus Doctoris Johannis Alphonsi de Fontecha, &c. Compluti 1611." Also described under the same name by Herrera, early in the seventeenth century—*De Essentia Causis, Notis, Præsagio, Curatione, et Præcautione Faucium et Gutturis Anginosorum Ulcerum Morbi Suffocantis,* GARROTILLO *Hispane appellati,* &c. Authore, Doctore Christophero Perez de Herrera, &c. Matriti, 1615.

IV. EPIDEMICUS STRANGULATORIUS—as it appeared in 1618 at Naples, the popular name of the disorder being "*male de canna,*" disease of the trachea—described by Nola Carnevale, Syambiti and others.

V. GULÆ MORBUS—as it was known in Sicily in 1600–25—described by Cortesius—"*Joannis Baptistæ Cortesii, Miscellaneorum Medicinalium Decades Denæ,* p. 696, Messanæ, 1625."

VI. ULCUS SYRIACUS—as it was seen in Syria and Cœlo-Syria, by Alaymus (*Marci Antonii Alaymi, Consultatio, pro Ulceris Syriaci nunc Vagantis curatione,* p. 54, 1632.)

VII. MORBUS STRANGULATORIUS — noticed in London in 1739–1746, by Dr. Forthergill—the title being "*An account of the Putrid Sore Throat,* by JOHN FORTHERGILL, M. D., pp. 32, 34. Fifth edition. London: 1769."

VIII. ANGINA SUFFOCATIVA — as described by Dr. Bard, of New York—his work being "*An inquiry into the nature, cause and cure of the Angina*

Suffocativa or Sore Throat Distemper, by SAM'L BARD, M. D."

Transactions of the American Philosophical Society, vol. 1, pp. 388, 404. Philadelphia: 1789.

IX. DIPHTHERITE—as described by M. Bretonneau, of Tours, in two memoirs, in 1821, also in 1825–26—as the disease appeared in different parts of France.

X. PSEUDO, MEMBRANOUS PHARYNGITIS, ANGINA PSEUDO MEMBRANOSA—as described by Churchill, "*Diseases of Children*," p. 468; Meig's *Diseases of Children*, p. 208, and other modern authors.

XI. DIPHTHERIA—of the nineteenth century.

SECTION II.

Remarks: History of the different Epidemics; Antiquity of the Disease.

In the whole range of disorders that the physician encounters, there is none more calculated to deceive the inexperienced practitioner—both as to its course and termination–than Diphtheria. Its ravages have made its name a dreaded word in civilized communities in all parts of the globe—the insidious nature of the complaint having rendered it the terror of parents and the dread of the medical practitioner.

Can there be to the mind of the humane man any thing more sorrowful, than the knowledge that tells of the certain and speedy death of a beautiful child who was but yesterday stricken with disease?

There she sits, her breathing (during her waking hours) not much impaired, playing with her toys, swallowing food and drink readily; nay, standing upright upon her feet, and moving as either inclination or command dictates. Yet Death has set his seal upon her brow. You know it from the appearance of the face; from a peculiar lustre in the bright blue eye; from the horrible rattling breathing while she sleeps; from the slight venous congestion in the cheek; from the alternate and almost periodical nature of the pains in the limbs; from the occasional ringing cough; and your duty calls you to reveal that which your feelings would gladly conceal—*Death*, certain and speedy--perhaps torturing, suffocating death.

Such cases are vivid in my mind, and I have been dismissed from the patient as forming a rash and harsh diagnosis—while others have been called whose more favorable prognosis for a time rekindled the dying hope, only to be suddenly and fearfully blotted out forever.

HISTORY.—For the last few years the medical periodicals have all been fruitful in papers, essays, etc., upon Diphtheria. Some of these possess much merit, and others are but the records of ordinary cases of diphtheritic sore throat, which usually prevail at the same time with true Diphtheria, and which may readily pass into the more malignant form of the disease.

Diphtheria is no new disorder in the literature of medicine, although it really is so to many medica practitioners of this century. It has made its appearance in many parts of the world, and has received the attentive observation and study of cultivated minds. Its great antiquity cannot be doubted. In the Fiske Fund Prize Essay upon Diphtheria,* Dr. Slade remarks, "That there is reason to suppose that we can trace back the history of this affection to a period almost cotemporary with Homer." Whether this be the case or not, certain it is that ten centuries after, we find distinct descriptions of a form of malignant sore throat in the writings of Aretæus, under the name of Egyptian or Syrian Ulcer.

At Rome, A.D., 380, a similar epidemic occurred, and to such an extent, that propitiatory offerings were made to the Gods: "Ut populus Romanus, morbo qui angina dicitur, promisso voto, sit liberatus."

In the years 1337 and 1557 the disorder prevailed in Holland; and in 1576 some parts of France were visited by the disease. According to Greenhow,† Fontecha, whose work was published in 1611, (vide section 1,) had seen the affection as early as 1581; and adds, that it prevailed as an epidemic in 1599 and 1600.

Villa Real records the presence of the disorder in Andalusia and other parts of Spain in 1590 and 1591.

---

* Diphtheria—Its Nature and Treatment. By Daniel Denison Slade, M. D. Philadelphia: 1861.

† On Diphtheria. By Edward Headlam Greenhow, M.D. Bailliere Bro.: 1861.

The earliest mention, however, is that made by *Aretæus*, who writes of its appearance in Egypt, Syria and Cœlo-Syria, and alludes to the fœtor from the mouth, the regurgitation of fluids through the nostrils, hoarseness and aphonia, which certainly are among the symptoms noticed.

According to Villa Real (who designated Diphtheria as *morbus suffocans*) hemorrhage from the nose and mouth was invariably fatal; and Herrera, speaking of the Spanish epidemic, describes eight varieties, which are said to correspond nearly to what has been observed during the present century. Of the epidemic which invaded Sicily, where the disorder received the name *gulæ morbus*, Cortesius notices the frequent occurrence of several fatal attacks in the same family; and Alaymus states that the invasion was most generally noticed upon the tonsils, or in the fauces, and occasionally in the nostrils.

A disease termed *morbus strangulatorius* had been observed in London in 1739, which continued periodically until 1746, when it broke out in an alarming manner at Bromley, in Middlesex, and at Greenwich. Dr. Fothergill published in 1748 "An account of the sore throat, attended with ulcers," which, from the description, evidently must have been diphtheritic in its character.* His pamphlet was the earliest notice of the disease that appeared in England. In 1747 *Ghisi* noticed an epidemic

* MM. Rilliet, Barthez and Greenhow concur in this view of the matter, although Churchill, in his Diseases of Children, p. 468, believes the disorder, described by Dr. Fothergill, to have been a species of gangrenous pharyngitis.

sore throat of a diphtheritic character prevailing at Cremona. A disease, resembling and designated *Croup*, appeared at Chesham in Buckinghamshire in 1793 and 1794, which, like the Cornish epidemic forty years earlier, appears to have been really idiopathic diphtheria.

In Sweden, an epidemic diphtheria appeared in 1755, where it raged for ten years. It was found in Stockholm in 1757-58; in Rasbo in 1761-62.

Dr. Samuel Bard, in a paper entitled "An Enquiry into the nature, cause and cure of Angina Suffocativa, or sore throat distemper," published in the Transactions of the American Philosophical Society in 1789, describes an epidemic disease, the nature and seat of which lead to the conclusion that it must have been Diphtheria, as it appeared in 1771 in New York. Greenhow quotes at length from this, but the limits of this chapter forbid any further mention save the insertion of a small paragraph, viz.: "Out of sixteen cases attended with *this remarkable suffocation* in breathing, seven died, five of them before the fifth day, the other two about the eighth. Of those who recovered, the disease was carried off in one by a plentiful salivation, which began on the sixth day; in most of the others by the expectoration of a viscid mucus."

The *New Hampshire Observer*, in 1828, published an account of a new and "curious disease," then prevailing, which has been supposed to be the same as that known by the name of Diphtheria. It was described as follows:

"Within the last three weeks, Mr. Alvah S.

Crafts, of Middelfield, has lost all his three children by a disease without a name in this country. The first symptoms show themselves in a cankerous humor near the root of the tongue; inflammation ensues, and the subject finally dies in all the agony of croup."

From these facts, it is plainly evident that Diphtheria is anything but a *new disease*, and that those physicians who state such news to their patients, or their students, are not certainly as well versed in the history of the disorder as they would have either their patrons or their pupils believe.

Again in this the nineteenth century the ravager stalked forth, slaying its hundreds and thousands, causing terror and dismay wherever it passed, awing the hardest hearts of the laymen, and stupefying, by its intractability, the most learned and scientific physicians. It would be needless in this work to enter upon the history of this last course of the disease. Interesting as the subject may be, the want of space alone would forbid further historical notice. It has been so prevalent that there are few who have not seen it—none who have not heard of it. In all the periodicals, both Allœopathic and Homœopathic, the symptoms are detailed; and the public journals have called the attention of the laity to the fearful nature of the affection by many notices of awful mortality.

Men read such paragraphs as these with terror:

DIED—In Etna, Tompkins county, January 1st, of Diphtheria, Emma Ophelia, aged 4 years and 6 months.

Also, January 2d, Prudence Eliza, aged 10 years and 17 days.

Also, January 4th, Hiram, aged 12 years, 5 months and 12 days.

Also, January 5th, Allen Benjamin, aged 7 years, 7 months and 20 days.

Also, January 6th, Pauline R., aged 20 years, 11 months and 10 days.

Also, January 8th, Polly Elizabeth, aged 18 years, 9 months and 22 days: all children of Daniel and Elizabeth M. Sherwood.

In another paper:

On the 11th instant, Henry, aged 13 years, 10 months and 4 days.

On the 12th, Edward, aged 14 years, 10 months and 3 days.

On the 17th, William, aged 4 years, 10 months and 11 days

On the 18th, Daniel, aged 9 years and 5 months.

On the 20th, Jacob, aged 10 years and 5 months.

All of Diphtheria. Children of Mr. Jacob Palmer, of Mountjoy Township, this county.

These paragraphs are inserted merely to demonstrate the devastation that may be made in a very short period of time, by the diphtheritic poison, and to show the great necessity of prompt remedial measures in its treatment.

In the next chapter, I shall give the disease as I have carefully observed it in many cases that have come under my own observation, as well as of those which I have seen under the care of my professional friends, and at the end of the work, when we come to an important point—the pathology of the disease—will be found the results of experiments and post mortem examinations, which may be of interest to all whose minds are interested in this important matter. After the description, a case or two in detail shall follow, for the benefit of the student.

I never shall forget the first case of Diphtheria that came under my own observation. It was in this city, (St. Louis,) 1859. I was called in consultation to see the disease at its advanced stage. I only heard the breathing, saw the suffocation, recognized the whistling cough and labored respiration, at once pronounced the disorder to be that of genuine membranous croup, and prepared to perform tracheotomy upon the little patient. I am thankful now, that the interference both of the family and my professional brother prevented the addition of the pain of a surgical operation to the sufferings of the little girl. Death was inevitable, and soon brought its relief.

CHAPTER II.—SYMPTOMS, DIAGNOSIS, &c.

Section I.

Semeiology of Diphtheria.

In the first stage of Diphtheria the symptoms are not much more marked than in the commencement of other acute diseases. The child—for generally children are those who suffer from the poison —is languid and uneasy, with a pulse quickened, but not extremely full, is restless and has not much appetite. These prognosticators of the coming affection may continue for some days, and be entirely without any appearance of inflammation of the fauces. Or, again, the parotid may enlarge and simulate mumps, or there may be stiffness of the muscles of the neck, or pains in the limbs, and often in the ear. The disease advances; anorexia continues; sometimes vomiting is present; the pulse becomes quicker but weaker. The throat upon examination is congested, and difficult deglution may be present, but the latter, according to my own observation, is by no means a pathognomonic sign. I have known children die of Diphtheria, who, from the first onset of the disease until it was very far advanced, had not the slightest difficulty in swallowing; and, in other instances, have observed that severe pain in deglution may be an early symptom, and may entirely disappear before death. Three cases are now vivid in my recollection, in the which, a few hours, nay, in one instance, a few minutes before a fatal termination, the patient swallowed morsels of food of considerable size. During these periods if the excrements be examined, the stools are found frequently covered with mucous, and the urine, in most cases, loaded with albuminous matter. Periodical and severe pains in the limbs are often present. An examination of the fauces (and in many instances this is by no means an easy matter) reveals patches of membranous exudation, very small, whitish or of a yellowish or a tawny hue, deposited mostly in the irregularities of the amygdalæ, and in the palatine arch, more frequently in the former than in the latter locality; the tonsils may be either enormously swollen, or not much enlarged. Salivation, which may have been noticed earlier in the progress of the disorder, continues: the pulse is still quick; the system generally announces that prostration which is so marked a feature in the whole course of the disease. A fœter is now noticed from the mouth—a fœter so peculiar that many physicians, and those, too, of high repute, regard it as pathognomonic of the disease. Dr. Ludlam* lays particular stress on this symptom,

* A Course of Clinical Lectures on Diphtheria, by R. Ludlam, M.D., p. 12.

and others have recorded cases wherein a diagnosis was made out by the peculiarity of the odor emitted from the mouth. The effluvia is *per se*–indescribable, but immediately recognized after having once become acquainted therewith. The diagnosis is then perfect, a case of true Diphtheria has commenced. The friends and relatives of the patient are anxious, the physician is aroused to the nature of the fearful adversary he has to encounter, and marks with watchful eye the progress of the complaint. If convalescence begin here, if the remedial measures properly chosen, appear to exercise a beneficent action, a refreshing slumber, a copious diaphoresis, a diminution of the swelling of the glands, an arrest of further membranous formation† and the gradual disappearance of that already noticed, a slower pulse and returning appetite, announce the welcome tidings: if otherwise, the symptoms are as plainly marked. Perhaps there may be no further increase in the exudation, but the nostrils begin to discharge a watery fluid. The eye—and that organ alone will often tell the tale, as it increases in its brilliancy and watches with never ceasing vigilance the motions of those who are fruitlessly endeavoring to soothe the anguish of the moment—is somewhat brighter; the face assumes a bluish, waxy appearance, resembling, to my fancy, the complexion of females when in the commencement of serious puerperal convulsions; the breathing is labored and rattling, always much worse when the patients attempt to

† For a description of the MANNER in which the exudation disappears, vide Section III of the present Chapter.

sleep; the voice is impaired; the exudation has considerably increased, and even invaded the roof of the mouth, and extreme prostration results. In such cases as these, there is still some hope, and such have made good their recovery. But the disease may advance notwithstanding every barrier that science and art can place to oppose its progress. The stridulous breathing increases, cough–a hollow, croupy, metallic, whistling cough—tells that the larynx is invaded. The discharge from the nostrils continues; fluids taken into the mouth return by the nose. The cheeks have here and there some slightly congested spots; an enlarged capillary vein spreading throughout their surface. Periodical and severe pains occur in the limbs; hemorrhage from the nose or mouth may be very troublesome; new and larger patches of false membrane are found upon the fauces. The labor of respiration continues; the patient grasps at the neck or the clothing to endeavor to gain air. The blueness of the face increases—that horrid ghastliness of countenance which, when once seen, is never forgotten—and death comes at last to end the fearful suffering. Or deglution may improve; the swelling of the glands subside; the membrane disappear from view; and just as those not conversant with this insidious form of the affection may suppose that improvement is about to commence, the sufferer sinks to death without a sigh or a groan, overwhelmed by the constitutional poison. Death by the latter method is certainly the most easy both for patient and attendant, for there is nothing more heart-rending than the imploring look of those who die from such torturing suffocation.

It is well for us to recollect that this coma of which we have spoken may be so extreme as to simulate death. This fact was forced upon my mind from the following sad circumstance:

In a neighborhood in which Diphtheria had prevailed to a considerable extent, a little girl was taken suddenly, and died in a very short time: the family fearing that some contagion might emanate from the body, rather hastened the funeral. After the child had been buried two days, a second in the family was attacked with the disease in its most malignant form, and soon succumbed to the poison. The parents desiring that both their children should occupy the same grave, had the former child exhumed. When the coffin lid was removed, the little one had altered her position—one hand was thrown up, and a stream of blood had trickled down from the nostril; these appearances giving evidence that interment had taken place before life was totally extinct. The horrible nature of the revelation may be imagined—and the physician should guard against such unfortunate results by carefully ascertaining that life no longer exists.

Section II.

Bretonneau's Diphtheria.

It may not be amiss, after noting the symptoms of the disease as they have come under our own personal observation, to record the characters of

Diphtheria, as described by M. Bretonneau, and published in 1826. He thus writes:

"At the beginning of the disease there is perceived a circumscribed redness, which is covered with semi-transparent coagulated mucus. This first layer, thin, supple and porous, may be still elevated by portions of unaltered mucous membrane in such a manner as to form vesicles. Often in a few hours the red patches visibly extend, step by step, through continuity or contact, in the manner of a liquid which is poured out on a plane surface, or which runs by striæ into one channel. The concretion becomes opaque, white and thick; it assumes a membranous consistence. At this period it is easily detached, and adheres to the mucous membrane only by very delicate prolongations of a concrete matter, which penetrates into the muciparous follicles. The surface which it covers is usually of a slight red tint, dotted with a deeper red; this tint is more vivid at the periphery of the patches. If the false membrane be detached, and leave exposed the mucous surface, the redness which appeared subdued under the concretion, reappears, blood transudes through the deep red points, the concretion reappears, and becomes more and more adherent upon the points first invaded; it often acquires a thickness of several lines, and passes from a yellowish white to a grayish and to a black color. At the same time the blood transudes with more facility, and constitutes those *stillicidia* which have been generally remarked by authors.

"Now, the alteration of the organic surfaces is

more apparent than at the beginning; often portions of concrete matter are effused into the substance itself of the mucous membrane; there is observed also a slight erosion, and sometimes ecchymosis in points which, by their situation, are exposed to friction, or from which the avulsion of the false membrane has been attempted. It is especially about this time that the concretions, which have become putrid, give out an offensive odor. If the concretions are circumscribed, the œdematous swelling of the cellular tissue immediately around makes the former appear depressed, and, judging from this appearance only, we might be tempted to believe that we had under observation a foul ulcer, with considerable loss of substance.

"If, on the contrary, they are extended over considerable surface, they become partially detached, and hang in shreds more or less putrefied, and simulate the last stage of sphacelus; but when we open the bodies of those who, several days sick, have succumbed to tracheal Diphtheritis, we shall find in the air-passages all the shades of inflammation from its first degree, as shown in the portions just invaded, up to that which has by its deceptive appearance led us for a moment to dread the supervention of gangrene."

Section III.

The Manner of Recovery.

Attention should be directed to the slow nature of the convalescence after severe attacks of Diphtheritic disease, and the peculiar manner in which this recovery may occur. A few years since, when we were not so far advanced, either in our knowledge of the disorder, or the remedial means that were most effectual in its treatment, it was impossible to observe many of the minutiæ which since have become quite well established. Among these peculiarities of recovery is, the *softening of the membrane*, which I affirm may take place in two very different ways: 1st. By actual decomposition of the structure, with fœtor and salivation. Or, 2dly, by its assuming a semi-fluid consistence, and being either expelled through the mouth and nostrils by expulsive cough, or ejected at will by the patient. I have seen recovery from diphtheritic disease by both these methods, and I would therefore call attention to the appearances presented.

Let us suppose a severe case of Diphtheria; such an one as is termed by many, malignant Diphtheria. The physician is called in the evening, finds the patient with high fever and slight congestion of the fauces, an enlarged parotid, and slight epistaxis. Diphtheria has been prevailing in the neighborhood, and is certainly suspected. The physician prescribes the appropriate medicines, and finds in the morning a *patch* of membrane from tonsil to tonsil: not a small isolated spot here and there, but a formation of from one to two inches in length. The patient, perhaps, is covered with an *uniform* redness in various parts of the body, and has screamed through the night with pains in the bones. The *same* medicines are continued, the practitioner understands his business and the disease which he would vanquish. Upon examining the fauces in the evening, the membrane has thickened and extended; the pulse is very quick; the breathing is so much impaired that the child can rest but a moment or thereabouts, and then starts up in his sleep with frightful dyspnœa. The rash has increased and the vigilance of the eye is well marked. Still, the well selected medicine is continued, and by morning, though there is no perceptible change in any symptom, yet there has been no *increase* in the exudation. Medicines are exhibited at longer intervals. In the evening, the peculiar odor has given place to the death-like smell of that putrefaction which occurs in living things. When the fauces are examined, the yellowish membrane has become darker and grayish, and has shriveled slightly around its edges. In twelve hours more, the odor has become so palpable that it pervades the whole room, and small particles of a dark, decomposed substance have been cast off. This process of mortification may continue until the whole exudation has been removed, accompanied with profuse salivation. In the second variety, a yellowish, slimy substance, about the consistency of thick starch, is expelled by coughing, both from the mouth and nose. It is often a matter of surprise to remark the immense amount of this peculiar semi-fluid which has been thrown off. It may accumulate in the cavities until it threatens suffocation, and then with a severe expulsive effort be ejected. A diagnostic mark I have observed is the following: That when recovery takes place by the latter method, the material which is thrown off possesses the *Diphtheritic odor*, while, as has been before mentioned, the decomposing process is necessarily accompanied *with fœtor.* These processes may occur also in the same patient. In the former cases I have often given the greatest relief to the sufferer by removing with the dressing forceps those portions of the exudation that appear friable and loose, recollecting never to use any *force* in such proceeding, as the *tearing* away of the membrane not only increases the tumefaction of the parts, but the raw surface in a few hours will *certainly become again coated with the exudation.*

SECTION IV.

Unfavorable Symptoms and Manner of Death.

There are certain symptoms which in Diphtheria must always be regarded as unfavorable, and too much stress cannot be laid upon their importance to the physician in his prognosis. And first of all in point of danger must be remembered—

The *invasion* of the *larynx* and trachæ as evidenced by the *croupy cough.* There are several varieties of cough that may be present in this disease; indeed, there are few cases that are not accompanied with a dry and somewhat irritating tussis; but the *ringing*, *rattling*, *croupy* sound, that tells of the invasion of the larynx may, so far as my observations and those of my professional friends tend, be laid down as almost invariably a *fatal* symptom.

2d. *Ulceration of and discharge from the nostrils.* This symptom may be present in the milder forms of the affection, but it must be regarded as unfavorable when the discharge is fetid and acrid to such a degree as to cause excoriation of those parts to which it is applied.

3d. *Hemorrhage from the nose and mouth.* When we consider the causes that are most likely to produce such hemorrhage, we cannot fail to perceive that the symptom must, in the majority of cases, be regarded as rather unfavorable in the prognosis. Certain children are more liable to epistaxis than others, and its recurrence in such will not be so unfavorable as in those who are not accustomed to such attacks, but in the majority of cases the hemorrhage is occasioned by necrosis of the blood and great anæmia, together with general prostration. Sometimes the bleeding is quite intractable, but from personal observation I am disposed to believe that a profuse hemorrhage that ceases, or can be controlled, is not as unfavorable as the constant trickling of defibrinated blood from the nose or the mouth: it is the latter variety that is the most unmanageable; and I have observed that when it is accompanied with great enlargement of the parotid gland, that the case has assumed a very unfavable aspect, although it may not be considered as entirely hopeless.

4th. *Coldness of the surface*, is another symptom that does not generally receive that attention which it deserves. The nature of the diphtheritic poison is such that it affects always, to a greater or less extent, the nervous centres, occasioning those symptoms of collapse among which we find the cold, clammy skin, which is so marked a feature in cholera and its typical diseases. Coldness of the surface in this disease generally indicates that the system is laboring under the most virulent diphtheritic poison, and even where it is unaccompanied by any other bad manifestations, should place the physician upon his guard, as trouble may certainly be anticipated.

5th. *Albuminuria*, will be noticed in another portion of this work.

Other symptoms are, diarrhœa and vomiting at an advanced stage of the disease; passage of the pseudo membrane per rectum; convulsions; petechiæ, rigors, etc.

Sudden death is by no means unfrequent. There are instances recorded of patients believing themselves much improved, who have walked a considerable distance, and then expired. In others, death has come so suddenly that medical advice has not been summoned at all, the post mortem examinations revealing the true nature of the disease.

Of those who succumb to diphtheritic disease, about an equal number die of suffocation and of zymosis, although many have been known to perish from exhaustion, from hemorrhage and convulsions. If the presence of the membrane within the larynx cause severe suffocative paroxysms, they are easily recognized, but if the gradual poisoning of the system is to terminate in death, a very different train of symptoms is manifest, and may tend to lead astray the inexperienced. The exudation may have become less in the fauces, the pulse and breathing perhaps be more regular, although the latter is still accompanied with the rattling noise, but the patient appears to be in a deep and perhaps quiet sleep, from which it is difficult to be aroused, but when fully awake is extremly bright and understands all that is said to him, but soon falls back into a state of stupor, which becomes more and more intense, may last from six to thirty hours, and will certainly terminate in death. There is no use, when such manifestations are present, to delude either oneself or the friends and family of the patient with the idea of recovery; such a course only tends to ultimate dissatisfaction to both parties.

"Death," says Greenhow,* "from syncope or the accession of collapse, fatal in a few hours after exertion, has so often happened when patients have appeared to be recovering satisfactorily, that convalescents from Diphtheria cannot be considered out of danger, until some time after the throat is well, and the very marked anæmia produced by the disease has disappeared."

Again, death may occur suddenly from cardiac spasms, or from imperfect closure of the valves of the right heart, the symptoms of which may easily be detected by auscultation. Such a case has very lately come under my personal observation. No

* Treatise on Diphtheria, p. 129.

autopsy, however, was permitted, and therefore the extent of the cardiac disorder could not be fully ascertained.

CHAPTER III.

Diagnosis between Diphtheria and other Diseases.

Although, as a general rule, the diagnosis of Diphtheria is not very difficult, yet there are cases that have come under my own observation, and from records, under the care of others, that have been somewhat perplexing, both to the medical adviser and to those interested in the care of the patient. Among these may be noticed—mumps, scarlet fever, croup, and gangrenous pharyngitis. In any one of these diseases the locality involved and the *presence of the false membrane is the pathognomonic indication*, together with the odor before alluded to.

Before however proceeding with any differential diagnosis, it gives me great pleasure to quote a most interesting and at the same time rather singular case from an interesting paper of my friend Dr. Ludlam, which was read before the Illinois State Homœopathic Association, in May, 1863.* He writes thus: "In exceptional cases, the only apparent local affection in Diphtheria will be found

---

* Vide Ludlam's Albuminuria in Diphtheria. N.A. Journal of Homœopathy, Vol. XII, p. 94.

in the kidneys. There is no doubt but this has sometimes been the cause of errors in diagnosis and consequent want of success in its treatment. To illustrate: A professional friend, who is no mean diagnostician, brought me a bottle of urine. 'This,' says he, 'is from a little patient whose case is an obscure one, and I want you to confirm or invalidate my diagnosis.' The urine was found to be slightly albuminous. The little floculi which were barely visible to the naked eye, and floated in great numbers in the fluid, proved, upon microscopical examination, to be pseudo-membranous in character, and the case was pronounced one of Diphtheria. * * * * * The reasons for the opinion that this child had Diphtheria, are the following:

1st. The peculiar eruption, which resembled that of rubeola in its general characters, while yet distinct from it.

2d. The sudden decline of the eruption without sequelæ.

3d. The pseudo-membrane in the urine.

4th. The specific curative effect of the Bi-chromate of Potassa upon the urinary symptoms."

It will be seen, therefore, that although the presence of the pseudo-membrane must be regarded as pathognomonic, yet we may be prepared to look for the presence of the exudation in other localities than the fauces.

Section I.

Differential Diagnosis between Parotitis and Diphtheria.

The preliminary symptoms of mumps and of Diphtheria, are, in many instance of a similar character, indeed they do not differ in their generality from the precursory manifestations exhibited by any acute disorder; there is chilliness and fever, general langour, indisposition and loss of appetite, with considerable thirst, and a coated tongue. After these symptoms have continued for some time, the others present, and it is worthy to remark how nearly the two diseases may simulate. The essential nature of parotitis is swelling of the parotid gland to a greater or lesser extent, the sub-maxillary glands also enlarging from sympathetic inflammation. In very many cases of Diphtheria a precisely similar condition of things may exist. Dr. Madden notices this fact, he speaks "of an unusual amount of swelling of the glands, the enlargement being quite as perceptible externally as internally."

Dr. Preston mentions several cases where there was great swelling of the glands of the neck.

Mr. Adams, of England, records cases in which the glands of the neck were much enlarged.

Mr. Moyce, of Rotherfield, in stating his own case, remarks: "There was much external swelling."

Dr. Bristow, in the report to the Pathological Society, of London, records a case wherein "there is great tumefaction, hardness and tenderness in the upper part of the throat, chiefly in the parotid and sub-maxillary regions, and more on the right side than on the left;" and, again, in referring to a post-mortem examination, says: "The parotid and sub-maxillary regions were much swollen and hardened, especially on the right side, where, also, the integuments were studded with congested and livid spots," and, again, in another case, "the external fauces on the right side are much swollen, very tense and tender, but not discolored."

Greenhow says, that great swelling of the glands is noticed, and is generally an unfavorable symptom.

Trousseau mentions enormous swellings of the glands of the neck as belonging to the worst forms of Diphtheria.

From these facts, therefore, we perceive that, in many cases of Diphtheria, the parotid gland may become much enlarged, thereby presenting the pathognomonic sign of parotitis.

Again, pain in the ear is often complained of by children affected with cynanche parotidea, and the same symptom is noticed in Diphtheria. M. Bretonneau mentions this symptom, and Dr. Beardsley, of Milford, Conn., has noticed that such suffering, in his section of country, was generally present. Here, again, a similarity exists: what, then, are the diagnostic symptoms? In Diphtheria we have the hollow, croupy, barking cough, with the peculiar breathing, particularly during sleep, but more especially the presence of the exudation itself, which may be revealed upon examining the mouth, or may be ejected during the cough.

Scarlatina and Diphtheria.

When Diphtheria first makes its appearance, it may be accompanied with a rash, resembling, in some respects, that of scarlet fever; and the occurrence of the two disorders together, even as epidemics, in the same localities, at the same periods of time, or the one succeeding or preceding the other, gave rise to the opinion that Diphtheria was but a modified form of scarlatina; in other words, the sore throat strongly developed on account of the non-appearance of the eruption. Another circumstance which favored this belief, was the presence of albuminuria in both.

The differential diagnosis between the diseases is well described in an editorial note to Dr. Preston's article on Diphtheria, which is so pertinent that we quote it entire. It reads thus: "Invasion, generally more insidious in Diphtheria, more violent and sudden in scarlatina (Valleix). It may, however, be *foudroyant*, and death has even anticipated the formation of false membrane. The swelling of the lymphatic glands of the neck, which is sometimes so enormous as to extend beyond the jaw, is altogether out of proportion to the intensity of the faucial affection. Join to this acute pain in the head, intense fever, excessive frequency of the pulse, and you have the signs of the onset of the worst forms of Diphtheria. Some hours after, you will observe false membrane on the uvula and velum, the discharge from the nose becomes fœtid, and if you open the nares with an ear speculum, false membranes are observed on the turbinated bones. The patient does not sleep, and is in a state of extreme agitation; the breathing is stertorous. After thirty-six or forty-eight hours, the features assume a livid pallor; delirium follows, and the patient dies with all the appearances of profound anæmia, and in a state of somnolent tranquility and prostration, strongly contrasting with the agitation which distinguishes the agony of croup." Death from scarlatina takes place from either congestion of the brain, engendering suffocation, or from the dropsy connected with the disease, while as has been before noticed, the patient in Diphtheria sinks to rest with adynamia or suffocation.

The albuminuria common to both diseases, occurs at different periods. In Diphtheria it appears very early in the course of the affection, while in scarlet fever it does not, as a general rule, manifest itself until the disorder is well developed, and the primary stages past.

Again, scarlet fever has its peculiar sequelæ in dropsy, congestions, suppurations; while Diphtheria also has its own; partial or total paralysis, inflammation of spinal cord, numbness, hemiplegia, &c.; and when to these we add that the pseudo membranous formation has been known to appear on cutaneous surfaces and wounds, there can be no doubt of the non-identity of the two diseases, and but little difficulty found in rendering, after careful observation, a correct diagnosis.

Croup and Diphtheria.

With reference to the diagnosis between croup and Diphtheria, Dr. Ranking, in his lectures, writes:* "The great distinctive mark between diphtherite and croup, properly so called, is to be found in the locality chiefly affected. In both, it is true, the main feature is the presence of an exudation, but in the one disease it commences in the fauces, and only reaches the windpipe by extension, and in a certain number of cases; in the other, that of true croup, it commences in the larynx and trachea, and does not necessarily affect the soft parts above the glottis. As a consequence of this, a marked difference is also found in the symptoms of the two diseases. In Diphtheria the uneasiness is first referred to the parts subservient to deglution; in croup, on the contrary, the earliest symptom is that of stridulous voice and breathing–a sympton which in the former indicates the final development of diseased action." There is, however, another distinction which should be remembered, and that is: in croup we believe the membrane to be distinctly *fibrinous*, while in Diphtheria it is *albuminous* in its character.† Again, we may notice a fact that bears some relation to

* London Lancet, January, 1859.

† Vide Chapter 3d, Section II.

these diagnostic facts, viz: that the exudation in croup sometimes exhibits a "well marked vascular arrangment, while that of Diphtheria appears incapable of organization."

There is another disorder which may, under certain circumstances, simulate Diphtheria, and that is *gangrenous pharyngitis*. In the former, there is no loss of substance, while in the latter, solutions of continuity are observed. In some instances there is but slight fever before the onset of the latter. The appearances of the false membrane are whiter in Diphtheria. In gangrenous pharyngitis the mucous membrane surrounding the ulcerated depression is of a darker and more purplish hue than the appearance noticed in Diphtheria.

Section II.

Divisions and Communicability, Causes, &c..

Physicians who have carefully observed the disease have described several varieties.

Dr. Madden, of England, in the British Journal of Homœopathy,* makes five divisions—the first distinguished by an enlargement of the follicles of the mucous membrane; the second, by swelling of the glands, highly congested condition of the mucous membrane, with ulcers surrounded by a red areola; the third, by the presence of a curdy deposit—which probably is the true diphtheritic disease in its beginning; the fourth, by difficult

* April, 1859.

deglutition, with swollen palate and adynamia; and the fifth, by the peculiar wash leather deposit and great prostration.

Dr. Dake, of Pittsburg, classifies his cases into six varieties;† and the Lancet Sanitary Commission, appointed to report on *Diphtheria*, make three distinct forms of the affection, viz.: simple, croupal and malignant Diphtheria.‡

My friend, Dr. Ludlam, of Chicago, writes thus: "Practically speaking, I am of opinion that we should recognize but *two* forms of this disease—viz., the simple and the malignant—*Diphtheria Simplex* and *Diphtheria Maligna*." Although, on page 86, he further says: "Under all its forms and varieties, the disease is essentially the same. In one family we may have pharyngeal, laryngeal, palpæbral, cutaneous and vulvular deposit of pseudo membrane". And he then quotes the following from Trousseau: "It is with Diphtheria as with variola, which, confluent or distinct, mild or malignant, is always variola."

It appears, however, that these distinctions really embarrass the beginner in practice, as the one may often assume strong features of the other varieties, or a single case may exhibit more or less of the peculiarities of all.

Certain it is, that when, upon examination, the buccal cavity presents an inflamed appearance, with swollen salivary glands and patches—be they ever

---

† N. A. Journal, Vol. X, p. 422.

‡ Science and Art, or the Principles and Practice of Medicine, p. 576.

so slight —of membranous formation, it behooves the physician to look well to his work, for trouble may be anticipated.

Diphtheria is generally conceded to be an endemic and epidemic disorder, not contagious, as a general rule, but subject, in its propagation, to those peculiar extesions and exarcerbations, which, in some instances, might lead to the supposition of its spread by contact. On this subject my friend, Dr. Dake, thus writes:

"1. There is a common cause or morbific influence, which pervades a particular part or region of country, resting equally upon all the inhabitants thereof. So far it is *epidemic.*

"2. There is a peculiar state or diathesis of constitution—a condition of health—which makes some of those inhabitants more susceptible to the *common* cause, or morbific influence, than others. So far the disease is *endemic*, or peculiar to certain persons.

"3. There are certain influences, such as sudden changes in the temperature or weight of the atmosphere, errors in diet, over-exertion of mind or body, which serve as *exciting* causes, which bring the common and *predisposing* causes more closely together, thus rendering them at once operative."

Dr. Preston, in an elaborate article on this subject, after discussing certain questions relative to the nature of the affection, thus writes:* "I conclude that Diphtheria is essentially an epidemic,

---

* United States Journal of Homœopathy, Vol. I, p. 236.

non-contagious disease, rarely, in certain favoring localities, becoming endemic by concentration of the epidemic influence." This is, no doubt, a fact, for there are few physicians who have paid attention to the subject, who have not, either from personal observation or from the perusal of medical periodicals, noticed several in one family, in one house, or in one particular locality, successively affected. I have in one instance seen five children attacked, in another four, and frequently two or three in the same family exhibit the diphtheritic exudation.

This, of course, would not prove the communicability of Diphtheria, although Bretonneau and others supposed the disease contagious by means of contact with the exudation, and not through the surrounding atmosphere. There are some facts that would tend to substantiate these premises, but there are many others that would contradict them. Dr. Leonard and Dr. Morris, while attending cases of Diphtheria, both suffered from a variety of ophthalmia, which they attributed to the contact of the exudation, which was thrown into their eyes by the spluttering of fluids from the mouths of the patients while undergoing local treatment. This is no proof whatever. If nitrate of silver, or perchloride of iron, or muriatic acid, be injected into the eyes, whether from the mouth or from a syringe, the probability is that ophthalmic symptoms will present. Greenhow says on this point, "Althought I have no proof that Diphtheria is communicable by means of the exudation, many facts have fallen under my notice which convince me that the disease is in some way or other communicable." One of these is very interesting—

"Diphtheria broke out in a Ladies' Boarding School at Whitham, in June, 1858, and proved fatal to one of the pupils; several others caught the disease, and the school was consequently dispersed. One pupil, who was considered convalescent, returned home to an isolated farm house at Foxearth, a parish on the borders of Suffolk, some miles from Whitham. At the time of her arrival she was still ailing, was voiceless, the tonsils were swollen and the posterior fauces congested. There was intense depression, and paraplegia supervened soon after her return, from which she slowly, but at length, perfectly recovered. On June 18, about a week after her return home, a sister, aged seven years, was found to be suffering from Diphtheria, and died within twenty-four hours. The following day another sister, aged seventeen, likewise fell ill, and died within three days. Four other cases of sore throat, with swollen tonsils, two of them attended with specks of exudation, occurred in the house about the same time. On the twenty-ninth of the month, the family removed to Lowestoft, where, it is alleged, that Diphtheria did not then exist; and soon after their arrival, two other children were seized, and died of the same disease. The malady did not extend beyond this household."*

Dr. Herpin, of Tours, and Dr. Gendron, of Chateau Loire, received the diphtheritic poison in the form of sputa upon the nostrils, and suffered

* Greenhow on Diphtheria, p. 87.

severely. Dr. Dyas cites the case of a boy having contracted cutaneous Diphtheria by using a bath in which a diphtheritic patient had been bathing.*

Dr. Ranking, whose lectures upon Diphtheria are worthy of perusal, and are deservedly held in high repute on this point, writes:† "My own conviction is, that it is infectious to a limited degree; by which, I mean, that when patients are accumulated in small, ill-ventilated rooms, the disease is very likely to be communicated; but I do not fear, that, like scarlatina or erysipelas, it may be propagated in spite of all sanitary precautions; still less that the infection can be conveyed by the clothes or persons of those who visit or superintend the patients. That it commonly spreads through the family once invaded, is to be attributed, in some degree, to the persistance of the same cause as originated the first case. What that cause is, it is difficult to determine." He then goes on to state that dampness, stench, and those causes usually the result of poverty, may be noted as those most likely to propagate the disorder; and although Bretonneau was of opinion that dampness certainly favored the spread of disease, I cannot quite agree with either—that is, I believe there is some other remote, and as yet undefined, cause of Diphtheria. The worst cases that have fallen under my notice were in those families who could procure all the conveniences of life; in some, indeed, the

* See Editor's Note to Preston's Diphtheria, U. S. Journal of Homœopathy. p. 236.

† London Lancet. January, 1857.

patients had, from birth, been accustomed to the comforts and luxuries that competence or wealth could procure. There can be no doubt that those means which always favor the spread of disease, as dampness, poor ventilation, bad food, improper attention to cleanliness, exposure, &c., will certainly influence the spread of this as well as other disorders; but, from my own observation and experience in the disease, I am convinced we must look elsewhere for the true causes of Diphtheria.

There have also occurred many sporadic cases of Diphtheria; and most physicians have heard of or witnessed cases of the disease, when there has been no prevailing epidemic.

I have now in mind an instance related to me by a gentleman of this city, in which his child, after being extremely ill for a number of days, and being given over to death by the physicians in attendance (who frankly stated their inability to form any diagnosis), ejected from the mouth and nostrils "a thick skin," as it was termed, which expulsion gave immediate relief, and the patient recovered.

This case occurred a number of years since, long before Diphtheria was generally known to the profession or the community.

CHAPTER IV.

Cutaneous Diphtheria, Concomitants, &c.

Before proceeding to record the actual concomitants of the disease of which we treat, it may be well to mention that diphtheritic deposits may take place on *cutaneous surfaces*, *wounds*, *ulcers* and *abraded surfaces;* also upon the schneiderian membrane, and within the vulvæ—a fact which certainly would disprove the position maintained by Sloan, that to the throat alone is the disease confined.

Some instances are worth recording.

"Mr. Edwards, of Wolverhampton, saw two cases of Vaginal Diphtheria, both of which proved fatal from exhaustion."

"Mr. Cooper, of Cromer, had, in one instance, seen the pudenda of a little girl covered with exudation, unattended by Diphtheria of the throat."

Dr. Nicholson, of Reddich, also reports a somewhat similar case.

The last-named physician, on the fifth day after an operation for *fistula in ano*, observed diphtheritic exudation upon the wound; and, in another case, having operated upon the soft parts adjacent to diseased bones, pseudo-membrane covered the wound, amputation was resorted to, but Diphtheria appeared upon the new wound, hemorrhage from the bowels supervened, and the patient died in fourteen days.

Other cases of this kind are upon record, but further repetition is here unnecessary.

Cutaneous Diphtheria is also not unfrequent. I have observed it in young children; in two instances, the diphtheritic deposit having formed beneath a vesicle upon the leg. This appearance may also be noted without any affection of the fauces.

Surfaces deprived of the epidermis are also prone to be the seat of the exudation. A case is reported of a child "who was suffering from extensive excoriation of the skin of the chest, produced by the constant dribbling of an acrid discharge from the mouth. When first seen, the whole of the inflamed surface was covered by a membranous concretion of firm consistence. The infant died in the course of the following day. No affection of the fauces could be discovered."*

I have noted in my own practice a rash in several instances—a miliary eruption upon the shoulders and back; in another case catarrhal opthalmia, and in another rheumatic and paroxysmal pains of great severity.

Dr. Dake† has recorded *rash*, *rheumatism*, *epistaxis* and *strangury*, as noticed by himself, concomitant with Diphtheria.

---

* Greenhow on Diphtheria, p. 119.

† N. A. Journal, February, 1862, p. 427.

SECTION I.

Eruptions.

There are a variety of eruptions that may present themselves in the different stages of the affection, and which are interesting to note both on account of their peculiarities, their varieties, and the parts of the body that may be affected. I have frequently noticed an uniform redness of the shoulders and upper part of the chest, both at the commencement and during the last days of severe diphtheritis. In other instances, regular scarlet fever may supervene and measles—the latter complication, from some reasons as yet unexplained, being the more dangerous complication of the two.

According to Valliex, the following is the diagnostic mark between the rash of Diphtheria and that of scarlet fever—the former is not followed by desquamation, while that of the latter is invariably superseded by exfoliation of the cutis.

"Diphtheria consecutive on measles and scarlatina, is often accompanied with bullæ or rupia simplex. As the bullæ become flaccid by absorption of their contents, a firm concretion may be felt beneath the still entire epidermis. This is found, on the removal of the covering, to exhibit all the characteristics of the diphtheritic exudation."*

In this connection, I would mention a rather

---

* Vide Editor's Note to Dr. Preston's Diphtheria. U.S. Journal of Homœopathy, Vol. I, No. 2, p. 236.

curious coincidence, which has lately been noticed, I attended two children for measles; they both did well until about the sixth day, when scarlet fever, of a malignant character, appeared in the one, and Diphtheria, in its worst form, attacked the other; both died, and both had been exposed to precisely the same contagious influence. The course of the Diphtheria in this case was extremely rapid. I discharged the child cured of the measles—through which she passed without an untoward symptom—on Thursday. On Saturday night, I perceived the first diphtheritic deposit; and on Monday morning she was a corpse. A third child was taken with scarlet fever, and recovered very slowly; a servant in the family also suffered from the same disease.

The existence of Small Pox and Diphtheria at the same time in the same system, was, for a time, a matter of doubt, but I have had, very recently, an opportunity of observing the two diseases developed simultaneously in the case of a young man of nineteen years. The pustules of the eruptive disorder were perfect and numerous, and the pseudo-membrane also exhibited as complete a formation as is ever found in diphtheritic disease.

Section II.

Hemorrhage.

Villa Real, who designated Diphtheria as morbus suffocans, has already, in years long passed, called attention to the fact of hemorrhages occurring concomitant with the disease, and its import in assisting to form a prognosis in the affection. As a general rule, the blood most frequently comes from the nares, although in some cases it has been observed to proceed from the gums, mouth, and rectum. It may be considered upon the whole as an unfavorable symptom, although in persons who have been subject to epistaxis, or in those of a hemorrhagic diathesis, it would not be regarded with the same degree of importance as in those who had never or rarely been obnoxious to such bleedings. When we take into consideration the peculiar defibrination of the blood that results in the more malignant forms of the disease, it is rather a matter of surprise that hemorrhages are not even of more frequent occurrence than they appear to be. Of the varieties of hemorrhage that take place, epistaxis is certainly the most frequent, bleeding from the buccal cavity next, and rarely, if ever, is proctorrhœa noticed.

I have seen these different varieties, and in different grades of violence, and so far as my experience goes, I believe that the passive hemorrhages are always the more dangerous, not on account of the loss of the vital fluid, but as exhibiting a more highly poisoned organism by the diphtheritic virus. A slight, but constant trickling of thin, watery, defibrinated blood from one or both nostrils, I have always found to belong to the worst cases of the disease; and in fatal cases the symptoms may frequently be observed.

Again, the hemorrhage which occurs late in the

progress of the affection, is indicative of more serious disturbance than a violent effusion of blood at the invasion; indeed, in the latter instances, it is not impossible that relief may be experienced from the discharge.

In many instances, these hemorrhages, be they active or passive, profuse or otherwise, are very difficult indeed to check, and in illustration we would here insert a case read before the St. Louis Homœopathic Medical Society, at its meeting in February, 1864, by my friend Dr. T. G. Comstock:

"On the 27th of Nov., 1863, at 9 P.M., I was called to see a female child of two and a half years, in the Lindell Hotel, attacked with what seemed to be spitting of blood, or at least hemorrhage from the cavity of the mouth. The mother's statement was: While she was at tea, the child being left in the care of the nurse, she had suddenly bled profusely from the mouth, she had also seemed all day somewhat unwell, and at times a little feverish.

"When I first saw her, she appeared only slightly feverish, the pulse was quick and somewhat excited, but she was apparently quiet until aroused by me to examine her, and then she was so irritable I could not examine the throat or cavity of the mouth. I saw the blood on the child's clothes in quite a quantity, and the nurse stated that it was at first coughed and spit up, and then that it trickled for some time from the mouth. Under the circumstances, I naturally concluded the bleeding must have come from the nasal passages, and regarding the case therefore as not in the least serious, prescribed—R. *Arnica*, 1st, every 2 hours.

"About 1 o'clock at night, I was called up, again to see the same child. The father informed me she was again bleeding from the mouth, and the throat was evidently very sore, and she could not swallow. He insisted his child was certainly near her end. I hastened at once to the bed-side of the little patient, and found that she really had bled a second time, and was still bleeding from the mouth.

"The source of the hemorrhage was to me the first question. I examined the throat, and found the tonsils very much swollen, looking very red, lacerated and spongy; one tonsil being covered with two or three small exudations evidently diphtheritic in character, and the other tonsil having only one upon it, and more or less blood still oozing from it. The posterior wall of the pharynx seemed also to be coated with a diphtheritic exudation or deposit. The child breathed heavily and swallowed with great difficulty; pulse 120, and fever decided, although not high. I had never before met Diphtheria complicated with these symptoms. The source of the hemorrhage was certainly from the tonsils. I ordered the tonsils touched at first with vinegar, which happened to be handy, and small pieces of ice to be given the child to swallow or melt in the mouth, according to the inclination of the patient; they were taken without difficulty, owing to the child's thirst. *Muriatic acid* and *Belladonna*, were given internally through the night. The next day she seemed better, having been very much relieved in her breathing; had no more hemorrhage, and could evidently swallow better; she appeared however very weak and languid, coughed a great deal, and rattled in the throat when breathing; the tonsils, palate and posterior wall of the throat looked much the same, except the sanguineous secretion upon the tonsils had disappeared.

"The same treatment was continued, and milk punch, with ice in it, was freely given. The second night, the child had a tranquil sleep for two hours or more, and on the morning of the third day seemed improved, and the throat looked better; still, a profuse secretion of a dark, greenish color could be seen behind the uvula. These symptoms continued much the same for nearly a week, the child being up a little on the fourth or fifth day, but fretful, languid and feverish at night.

"The swelling of the tonsils had abated somewhat on the third day, when *Deutoiodide of Mercury* was given instead of *Muriatic acid* in alternation with *Belladonna;* but, on the sixth day, *Hepar Sulphur* was given for two days, and this followed by the *Muriated tincture of Iron*, four drops, three times daily. The child remained somewhat languid, but the appetite improved a little, and on the twelfth day she was quite well.

"According to Villa Real, in Diphtheria, hemorrhage from the mouth or nose always proves fatal. As this was the first case of the kind I have ever met with, I desire to record it, and inquire of my professional brethren if they have observed similar cases?

"I have seen (May '64) two cases of hemorrhage in Diphtheria, since the report of the above case. One case of a boy at 5, had a dangerous attack of the disease; hemorrhage from the nose and mouth took place on the sixth day of the attack—the child recovered entirely at about the ninth day.

"In another case of apparently the mild form of the disease, bleeding from the nose set in on the seventh and tenth days. This was readily controlled, but the child died on the seventeenth day. We consider hemorrhage in Diphtheria as a very serious complication; and Dr. Jacobi, in the *Amer. Med. Times*, Vol. I, p. 114, speaks of it as such.

"The remedies for this form of the disease are: *Ol. Terebinth.*, *Arnica*, *Hammamelis* and *Crocus*. As to the remedies applied locally, such as *Muriated tinct. of Iron*, *solution* of the *Per-sulphate of Iron*, *Alum*, *Ol. Terebinthinæ* and *Creosote*, we sometimes resort to one of them; but limit ourselves to one or two or perhaps four applications; if, after this, the exudation still forms, we use no local applications other than salt and water, or claret wine and pounded ice, as I am convinced that stronger preparations, persisted in, can do more harm than good.

"In some cases of Diphtheria where the convalescence is protracted and the patient enfeebled, we have used with the best success *Pyro-phosphate of Iron*. It is, withal, the pleasantest, safest, and most agreeable of any of the ferruginous preparations, and seems to possess more analeptic properties than the muriated tincture, protoxide, or the carbonate. It is perfectly soluble in water, and I have found no child over two years old refuse to take it. It may be given in solution. R. *Aq. distill.*, oz. ij.; *Pyro-phosphate of Iron*, grs. xv. M. *et ft. sol.* Dose, from a half to one teaspoonful every three hours."

Section III.

Other Concomitants.

Rheumatism.—Rheumatic affections, of the most serious character, sometimes accompany the disease, and the attacks of pain are generally periodical in character.

Pleuro-Pneumonia.—Inflammatory action has been known to extend along the larynx and trachæ to the lungs; and both single and double pneumonia have been found coincident. Phrenitis has also been noticed by observers, and has in cases proved not only a very obstinate, but in some instances a fatal complication.

Venous Congestion.—There is scarcely a malignant case of Diphtheria which does not, in some of its stages, present appearances of this kind on some portion of the surface of the body. I believe that the peculiar mottled, bluish, or indeed sometimes purplish hue of the cheek, that is sometimes observed, even in the first stages of the affection, is always a serious symptom, and one indicating approaching trouble. It arises from the thorough contamination of the venous system by the poison, and a patient cannot be too closely watched who presents the appearance in question. It is rather a remarkable fact that so many acute observers of the disease have overlooked this symptom, which is certainly often present in malignant diphtheritic disease.

CHAPTER V.—SEQUELÆ.

The majority of the sequelæ of Diphtheria are those belonging to the nervous system; perhaps, three-fourths of all the complaints that follow severe diphtheritic disease can be traced to the action of the virus upon the nerve centres, all tending to impress upon the mind the profoundness with which the human system may be affected by the poison, and serving to illustrate the difference of diagnosis between the disorder in question and others, which in their premonitory or later symptoms may bear to each other quite a striking similitude. It is astonishing also to observe the tendency that the glandular system appears to exhibit during convalescence, to *suppuration.*

In my own practice, I have observed many of the latter, particularly suppuration in glands, and in the cavities of the nose and ear, also of the lungs; and have also observed aphonia, sometimes complete, sometimes partial, with great prostration, continue for weeks after a severe invasion.

Convulsions.—Cases are upon record where most violent enclampsia has been present during the course of the disease—a most distressing and prolonged case of the kind having fallen under the care of my friend Dr. Temple. The records of the whole case have been published in the *Western Homœopathic Observer.*

Mr. Gravely, of Newick, mentions the case of his own son, aged two years, in whom singular paralysis of the muscles of the neck occurred; the head rolled about by its own weight in all directions, and, when once fixed, appeared immoveable.

In two cases under my own supervision, the head has been drawn to one side, and remained in such position from one to several months.

Impaired vision has also followed the disorder, cases of which Greenhow records, and which very recently I have observed, accompanied with a peculiar nasal twang of the voice—supervening upon one of the most violent attacks of Diphtheria which it has yet been my fortune to witness.

Aphonia.—Perhaps this symptom is the most common of all the diphtheritic sequelæ, and is indeed often difficult to overcome. In several instances, patients have been known to lose the voice for weeks and months together, and in others a singular *paralytic condition of the muscles of the palate* has been observed, which almost entirely prevented deglutition of liquid aliment.

Strabismus.—Squinting, both of the convergent and divergent varieties, often occurs, but I believe is not generally a permanent symptom.

Dr. J. F. Merrit, of Staatsburg, New York,* mentions a case of Diphtheria following erysipelas after vaccination; and very many have noticed affections of the spinal marrow as sequelæ of the disease.†

M. Roger has investigated the history of the numerous cases of diphtherite which have occurred during 1861, in the Children's Hospital, at Paris, for the purpose of ascertaining the relation of paralysis to this affection. Of 210 cases thus observed, paralytic accidents have appeared in 31, or in about one-seventh of the whole number; but, as many of the patients are removed from the hospital before the period of paralysis arrives, and as many also die early of the diphtheritis, the proportion is probably much greater; in fact, about one-fourth. M. Roger also found that secondary paralysis is rare after other acute maladies. Diphtheritic paralysis appeared most frequently between the ages of four and six; 21 times in the female, and 17 in the male sex. The season of the year did not appear to have any influence over it. The paralysis almost always began at the pharynx and soft palate; in 2 out of 10 cases, the paralysis reached the lower limbs.‡

Dr. Dake notices as sequelæ—coughs, glandular abscesses, otorrhœa, ozœna, erysipelas and paralysis.

---

* North American Journal of Homœopathy, No. XXXIX, page 485.

† For an interesting cure of such a case, see U. S. Journal of Homœopathy, August, 1861.

‡ American Medical Times: New York, 1862.

The most peculiar and the most frequently recurring sequela is the *peculiar prostration* that remains after a severe attack of the disease; and this is so well marked as to deserve especial attention of the practitioner. All the movements of the body are uncertain and tottering; the skin assumes a peculiar pallor; the muscles of the tongue appear to lack the power they should possess; severe pains occur in the limbs; strabismus may be present; the hearing be impaired; and, in fact, idiocy threaten the patient.

The presence of albumen in the urine will be noticed in the chapter upon pathology, where, according to the ideas of the author, it properly belongs.

To illustrate the course of the disease, and its sequelæ, the following case of rare interest is appended, because surgical treatment was necessary and efficient in the treatment, and because the pyæmia which resulted was remarkable from the immense amount of pus that was discharged, and the number of times that paracentesis was resorted to for the relief of the patient.

On January 14th, I was called to visit a child, aged between three and four years, who had been suddenly attacked with symptoms of convulsions. I found the little patient almost comatose, with burning red cheeks, glistening eyes, slight dyspnœa, pulse 130, and at irregular intervals some twitches of the facial muscles. Supposing that, as on the evening previous there had been a large company at the house, the symptoms resulted from dietetic transgression, I prescribed *Belladonna* 3°, and *Ipecac* 6°, in solution, to be taken every fifteen or twenty minutes, and promised to return in an hour or two. Upon my arrival, the patient had improved in appearance, but was much prostrated, and complained of some difficulty of deglutition. Upon examination, the throat presented appearances unfavorable to a speedy termination of the ailment. The right tonsil was swollen considerably, and covered with patches of diphtheritic formation, which at once placed the diagnosis beyond a doubt. R. *Merc. protiod.* 3°, a powder every two hours. Visited the patient at 11 o'clock, P.M. Pulse quick and small, the amygdalæ covered with false membrane, which had extended itself to the anterior lateral half arches of the palate. There was great redness of the tongue and mouth, together with much difficulty of breathing, accompanied with that peculiar rattling-whistling sound that is so alarming to the friends of a patient, and so full of meaning to the physician. The right tonsil had increased enormously in size, and in itself appeared to threaten complete suffocation. Blueness of the face, stridulous breathing, and convulsive movements of the chest, indicated plainly that the little patient could not long survive, if some very prompt measures were not immediately resorted to. Indeed the family had given up all hope, and considered the boy already in a dying condition. After a little consideration, although the false membranes were obstructing the air passages to a certain extent, I concluded that the tonsil was also greatly increasing the dyspnœa, and that its excision would allow time for the medicines to act, and might also remove a portion of the exudation. I accordingly took off a portion of the amygdalæ, and was gratified to perceive evident temporary relief. Ordered a desert spoonful of beef tea to be administered every hour, and presented the first trituration of the *Chlorate of Potash* in water, a teaspoonful every half hour.

Was summoned again at 5 o'clock, A. M., and found the exudation increasing, the breathing more impeded, pulse more depressed, but very quick, and every symptom becoming aggravated. I then determined to try the treatment of Dr. Madden, as published in the *British Journal of Homœopathy*, and, with some difficulty, succeeded in touching the exudation with the tincture of the *Muriate of Iron.* It was noticed that, wherever the solution was applied, the edges of the isolated portions of the diphtheritic formation appeared to shrivel; and in about an hour, a quantity was thrown off. R. *Ammonium causticum* 1° (in solution); a teaspoonful every half hour.

Upon my return later in the morning, although no improvement was manifest, still the symptoms had not increased in violence. A nutritious diet was recommended, and the same medicine continued, at longer intervals. In the evening, the topical application was renewed, and the *caustic Ammonia* still prescribed. At twelve o'clock at night I visited the patient again, and found the breathing about the same, exudation not increased, and the prostration very great. At this juncture,

I prescribed the *Iodide of Arsenic* (a preparation lately brought to my notice by Dr. Weeks, of Boston, and highly recommended by him in the treatment of cancerous formations, whether schirrus or the open sore,) and the result was surprising. Although this medicine was used empirically, yet, judging from the pathogeneses of *Iodine* and of *Arsenic*, and from the very beneficial action of the combinations of *Mercury* with *Iodine* in these affections, I was led to suppose that the preparation might prove serviceable in this case. My expectations were not disappointed. From this time, the boy began to improve—slowly, to be sure, and without appetite, except a peculiar and almost insatiable desire for gravy. He would eat nothing else; and although cautioned to the contrary, his nurses, supposing that all danger had passed, and allowing their feelings of affection to bias their better judgment, frequently allowed him rich gravies and hashes, of which he often partook freely. Notwithstanding this, however, he began to walk about, and my mind was for a time relieved from the anxiety in reference to a case that had so perplexed me. This improvement was but temporary. Great sleeplessness, for several weeks, was the first sentinel that warned of approaching danger. The child appeared quite comfortable through the day; but the livelong night there was no rest, either for the nurses or patient. I could discover no cause for this, excepting unwholesome food, and therefore restricted the diet to the plainest and most nutritious articles; recommended rides into the surrounding country, and prescribed the ordinary medicines for insomnia; but there was no improvement. There came on profuse night sweats, with that bright circumscribed red spot upon the pale and wan cheek that marks the progress of the life-destroying hectic. Emaciation was gradual, but steadily increasing; and it was evident that although there were some days of temporary improvement, yet, on the whole, the patient was rapidly approaching the grave.

Up to this time, phthisis was suspected; but the cough was not that of consumption. The chest and abdomen were measured from time to time, to ascertain an increase or diminution in size. There was a certain indistinctness of the respiratory murmur on the left side of the thorax; and about in the locality of the lower lobe of the left lung, no sound at all could be detected. Bronchial respiration was present, and on percussion there was dullness on the anterior and left lateral wall of the thorax. The patient could only lie on the left side, a change of posture to the right bringing on a short cough. With all these symptoms, there were constant acute pains in the hips and shoulders. From these manifestations the diagnosis was, the existence of fluid within the thoracic cavity; but whether this fluid was serous or purulent, it was a difficult matter to determine correctly. However from the hectic and sweats, (although such symptoms are noticed in hydrothorax,) I concluded that pus was forming, and ordered warm unmedicated poultices to the side, and by so doing endeavored to make the abscess, if such it was, point at the intercostal spaces. The child, however, continued to lose ground daily, and it was thought that perhaps the thorax might cautiously be opened by the application of the *caustic*—a method preferred by many excellent surgeons at the present day; but as yet there was no perceptible fluctuation, and the difficulty of positively determining the character of the fluid remained the same. The *caustic Potash* was used daily for three days, but with no success, and the little emaciated sufferer complained so bitterly of the pain consequent upon its application that I determined to hazard the operation. During the last few days of the treatment, the swelling on the left side of the thorax had become rather more prominent, and it was very evident that the life that had been ebbing away for months was very soon to terminate.

On Thursday, the 10th of May, I visited my patient as usual, in the morning, and informed the family that, at 12 o'clock (noon), the operation of paracentesis would be performed. To this procedure objections were raised by some members of the family, they being unwilling that the patient should undergo any farther treatment.

Drs. Temple and Adams accompanied me to the house at the time appointed, and found the patient in a sinking condition. Indeed, the breathing was difficult, there was scarcely any pulse, and that weak and intermittent, and the voice was altering to such an extent that the expediency of the operation was doubted. However, after some consultation, I passed a trocar between the last true and first false rib, and had the satisfaction of seeing *pus* discharge through the canula. The flow at first was not very profuse, but by withdrawing the canula, it passed out in quite a stream. About three teacupfuls were discharged, when, from the exhausted condition of the patient, it was deemed best to allow him to rest. He was laid upon his back, and fell into a quiet slumber, such an one as the poor little fellow had not known for months. He wakened in about two hours, asked for nourishment, and passed a good night. In the morning, however, a violent cough was presented, and upon examining the wound, it was found closed. I opened it again, and about four teacupfuls of matter of the same character was discharged during the day. Throughout this period, the medical treatment consisted chiefly in the exhibition of *Arsenicum*, *Calendula* and *China.* The cough was not much relieved, and the suppuration for a week was so profuse as to threaten life once more. Upon referring to a paper published in the *British Journal of Homœopathy*, on the effects of *Iodine* injected into serous cysts, and from the analogy of the cases therein mentioned, and the great success of *Iodine* injections after the operation for hydrocele, it was concluded to try the expedient. I therefore injected a solution composed of one part of *Iodine* to four of water into the cyst, at two different periods, and although the irritation and pain were for some moments considerable, yet, during the day, the pus became changed in character, while the cough was rather increased. From that date until June 3d, the medicines prescribed were *Sulphur*, *Iodine* and *Silicia*. Under this treatment, the discharge became much less, and the appetite partially returned; the cough, however, continued; the discharge became fœtid, and in the middle of June was evidently on the increase. The child lingered until the 3d day of July, when it gradually sank to rest—his body worn to a skeleton, but his mind perfectly clear, and his eye extremely bright. This case is given entire, as it is one of much interest, and one which also will prove the terrible extent to which the system may be involved by the diphtheritic poison.

CHAPTER VI.—PATHOLOGY.

To the educated Homœopathic physician, the pathology of a disorder is always a point of interest; and, as thus far, the pathology of Diphtheria is by no means fully established, it behooves each physician to render his own observations, as compared with that of others, in order that in time a correct appreciation of the subject will result.

The following post-mortem appearances were carefully observed by the author with reference to the proper elucidation of various points in the pathology of the affection; and they are offered to the profession, not by any means as establishing the true nature of the disease, but as absolute facts from which, perhaps, correct deductions as to the nature of Diphtheria may be drawn.

SECTION I.

Post-Mortem Examinations.

AUTOPSY I.—Performed March 17th, 1860. The subject, an infant (one of twins), had died within three days, of malignant Diphtheria. The usual incisions, to expose the trachea and larynx, were made, the sternal muscles divided, and the thyroid body brought to view, and turned aside. A longitudinal incision was then made through the anterior face of the larynx and trachea, the mucous lining of the passages being thus exposed. A circumstance here occurred which for a time caused some perplexity of mind: so soon as the knife had penetrated the cartilaginous rings of the trachea, a watery fluid gushed from the wound. This transudation was sanious and frothy in character, and, floating in it, small particles of membrane were noticeable. The membrane had partly covered the inside of the larynx, and was greatest on each alæ of the thyroid cartilage. Some patches were noticed lower down on the cricoid; but none within the trachea, although the lining membrane of that tube presented high inflammatory appearances. Within the sacculi laryngis, (the ventricles of Morgagni,) there was a much more tenacious deposit. This examination was not satisfactory, as it was made in some haste, and the fear of marring the appearance of the body prevented the incisions being sufficiently extended to bring fully into view either the trachea below or the rima-glottidis above. The adynamia in this case was probably the cause of death; but the escape of so much fluid from the windpipe, and the increased deposit within the ventricles of Morgagni, made an impression upon my mind.

Autopsy II.—On the 24th day of August, 1861, a second opportunity offered for an examination.

There was immense tumefaction of the parotid and sub-maxillary glands, the latter so much enlarged as almost to fill the whole digastric triangle. The number of veins branching from the inferior thyroid, with an anomalous course of the anterior jugular, also were worthy of remark. The thyroid gland was swollen to a size considerably greater than usual, and appeared to be rather softer than natural. In this instance, I resolved to take out the trachea and larynx, instead of allowing them to remain and exposing their interior by a longitudinal incision—a course pursued in the last autopsy. By such method, besides submitting the air passages to a more minute examination, I might extend the inquest to the mucous lining of the œsophagus. Dissection was therefore made above the hyoid bone, and the palato-pharyngeus and palato-glossus muscles divided as high up as possible. The posterior wall of the pharynx was then cut through, and the structures thus loosened drawn forward and dissected from the faces of the vertebræ as low down as possible, and then both trachea and œsophagus divided and withdrawn. During this dissection, as soon as any part of the trachea or larynx was opened, a fluid, similar in character with that observed in the first post-mortem examination, was thrown off; but the quantity was very much greater than was noticed in the former case. The larynx and trachea presented the following appearance: the exudation had almost disappeared from the lateral half arches of the palate, and the uvula was free, but directly anterior to the epiglottis, there was a great deposit of false membrane; the mucous surface was almost obliterated, and the epiglottis itself, instead of standing upright, was thrown partially backward over the rima-glottidis. A division was then made longitudinally of the œsophagus from behind, and it was found in a healthy condition. The trachea and larynx were then cut through from below, upward, on the posterior face of the tube, through the large diameter of the cricoid cartilage. The membrane that covered the arytenoid cartilages was tumefied and purple; the vocal chords could not be all seen, for the coat of exudation; but there was no trace whatever of membranous formation within the trachea. The examination ended here, no other organs being subjected to investigation, because the body of the child had already been laid out, and the hour of burial was close at hand.

Autopsy III.—Conducted on the morning of the 15th February, 1861, one of the graduates of the college assisting in its details. I was very anxious to ascertain if the ideas that had forced themselves upon my mind from the two other examinations which I had made in reference to the peculiar locality of the deposit would be verified in this instance, and therefore determined to conduct the investigations with greater care. The incision was made in the mesial line of the neck, from a point immediately between the tendinous origin of the sterno-cleido-mastoid up to the genio-hyo-glossus muscle; the latter was then divided transversely at the base of the tongue. The genio-hyoid muscles were detached at the hyoid bone, and the sterno-thyroid, thyro-hyoid, and sterno-hyoid muscles turned aside. With this dissection, so far, there *was no transudation:* all the parts were healthy, the thyroid body was in its usual position, and the course of the inferior thyroid vein and superior thyroid artery were normal. Proceeding as before, I then divided transversely the trachea and œsophagus, without injuring the great vessels below, when immediately there flowed forth *the fluid* which has been already referred to. Dr. Walker will bear me witness, I think, that there must have been a pint of thin, frothy, putrid transudation poured out from the divided extremity of the trachea. This should have been preserved and experimented with; but unfortunately, in this instance, it was not. The trachea, the larynx, and the hyoid bone, with the epiglottis, was then taken out, and, upon examination, the membrane was found so thickly deposited upon the anterior face of the epiglottis and in the depressions of the glosso-epiglottidean folds, that the rima-glottidis was contracted to a small slit, which was further encroached upon by the œdema of the parts. The trachea and larynx were then divided from behind, and the layers of thick tenacious membrane that lined the wings of the thyroid cartilage were truly surprising. *No vocal chords were visible*, and the sacculi between them could not be distinguished until the membrane had been withdrawn with comparative force. No trace of exudation was found in the trachea, though the lining membrane thereof bore marks of inflammatory action.

These examinations had made considerable impression upon my mind, and I was anxious that another occasion should offer, when I could make further investigation into the pathological states exhibited after death by Diphtheria. The desire also to obtain some of the transuded fluid, if it should occur again in other dissections, was quite insatiable. Here, in three autopsies, I had witnessed after death the fluid that has been mentioned; had found the most deposit on the anterior face of the epiglottis, and in the ventricles of Morgagni; and I wished to ascertain if the false membrane was generally located in these parts.

AUTOPSY IV.—This post-mortem examination took place on the afternoon of the 2d of March, Dr. Luyties assisting. The incision was made from the insertion of the genio-hyoid muscles to the extremity of the ensiform cartilage. The origins of the sterno-cleido-mastoid were divided, the muscles on the anterior face of the windpipe dissected back, and the sternum removed. By passing the scalpel upward and backward (dividing the muscles connecting the hyoid bone with the tongue), we separated the anterior and posterior lateral half arches of the palate, and divided the pharynx. The next incision was made above the left innominata vein, transversely across the trachea and œsophagus. Here, again, we noticed the escape of the fluid, somewhat thicker in this instance, on account of the admixture of a little venous blood, which escaped from the inferior thyroid vein, that was necessarily cut across ; but still so profuse that we were obliged to absorb it before proceeding with further dissection. Some of this transudation I preserved for experiment. Drawing forward the trachea and œsophagus, they were taken out, and presented the following appearances: a pseudo-membranous growth was firmly attached to the glosso-epiglottidean folds, which had, as in the third case detailed, pressed backward the epiglottis. This cartilage itself was much swollen, very convex on its anterior aspect, with a corresponding concavity on its laryngeal side. In this cavity was a deposit of false membrane more tenacious in character than any I had previously had an opportunity of observing. The œsophagus was then divided by a longitudinal incision on the posterior face of the tube, and the mucous lining thereof wes found somewhat thickened, though presenting no trace of inflammatory action. The windpipe was then laid open also from behind, and the exudation was found to be in positions similar to those noticed in other examinations, viz.: on the alæ of the thyroid, and particularly in the ventricles of Morgagni. These sacculi could not be at all perceived until, with the forceps, I drew out the membrane that completely filled them. The covering of the arytenoid cartilages were much swollen, the tumefaction extending throughout the whole rima-glottidis. There was but slight trace of inflammation in the trachea; indeed, none beyond the two or three superior rings of the tube. The lungs were much collapsed and very white in appearance, but became somewhat darker after they had been exposed for an hour to the atmospheric air. In many lungs that I have had an opportunity of examining, such great and peculiar pallor has not been observed. The pericardium was natural in appearance, and it contained fluid rather greater in quantity and more dense than usual. The heart was then taken from the media-steinum, by dividing the great vessels high up; and as we raised it from the body, a slight shred hanging from the aorta attracted attention. This was so unusual that, following an impulse without thought, I drew it out. It measured, as I have since ascertained, two inches in length, and an eighth of an inch in breadth. How far it extended within the left ventricle, my thoughtless act, of course, prevented me from ascertaining. The cavities were next examined; and inserting the scissors below the opening of the inferior cava, we divided the wall of the right auricle, in the course of the sculcus transversalis. Upon exposing this cavity, an object of intense interest presented itself. A mass of substance resembling a polypus filled nearly the whole auricle; was somewhat firmly attached to its walls, and sent shreds or processes, if we may so term them, between the musculi pectonati of the appendage. But surprise did not end here. This abnormal formation extended into the right ventricle (the external wall of which was now carefully divided), through the ostium venosum, preventing the proper closure of the tricuspid valve, and was firmly attached to the columnæ carneæ. It was also adherent to the extreme tip of the ventricle, and then followed a direction upward toward the pulmonary artery. The ventricle was then laid open by another longitudinal incision, and, extending to the semilunar valves, this peculiar structure continued; or, perhaps, to give a more definite idea of its position, the foreign substance was V-shaped, with the apex pointing to the extremity of the ventricle, and extending downwards from the auricle to the tip of the ventricle, and upwards to the valves guarding the pulmonary artery: in other words, it followed the exact course of the current of venous blood within the right heart. The left auricle and ventricle, with the valves, were normal, and nothing unusual was presented in them excepting the shred of membranous formation, which has already been noticed.

The whole heart, with its contents, weighed two ounces and two drachms. It measured five and a quarter inches around the auricles, and three and a quarter inches from the top of the right auricle to the tip of the ventricle on the same side. From the margin of the tricuspid valve to the extremity of the right ventricle, the space was about two and one-eighth inches. The curious formation within the cavities measured two and a half inches downward from auricle to ventricle, and two and three quarter inches upward to the semilunar valves. Its greatest transverse diameter, of course, was within the ventricle, and measured a little over three-quarters of an inch. The larynx, trachea, œsophagus, and hyoid bone weighed one ounce, and the membrane exuded twenty-nine grains. The spleen was much smaller than normal, and the remaining intestines, although not subjected to a critical examination, were apparently healthy.

From these post-mortem appearances, we may infer that the disorder seldom extends itself to the œsophagus; that, in the majority of cases treated as Diphtheria and reported cured, the affection has not extended very low down into the air passages, and that such extension is certainly a most dangerous complication. These ideas are also to a degree confirmed by the experience of others in the profession.

It is not, however, at all necessary that the trachea should be involved to produce death; for, in the instances recorded, there was no false membrane found within that tube, and in some, but very slight inflammatory action was noticed. *The chief points of deposit I believe to be, first, the tonsils, then, the pouches formed by the three folds of mucous membrane as it is reflected from the base of the tongue upon the epiglottis, and thirdly, the ventricles of Morgagni or sacculi laryngis.* In the cases which I have examined, the exudation was invariably found in these localities—in the one instance, to such a degree as to shut down the valve of the larynx, and in another, to pull it backward to a considerable extent. When, moreover, we recollect the hoarseness and aphonia that remain for weeks and months after patients have recovered from the severer forms of the disease, the presence of deposit and great unhealthy action between the chordæ vocales cannot be doubted.

Similar observations have been made by others. Greenhow writes: "The epiglottis besides being covered above and below, or on both sides with exudation, is likewise *often* swollen so as to contract the entrance of the windpipe."

Dr. Sanderson found, in an autopsy performed by him, the upper surface of the tongue healthy as far back as the *base of the epiglottis*, where there was found a small path of exudation. The mucous membrane of a cavity behind the left tonsil (pillar of the fauces) contained a creamy exudation.

Mr. Simon found the membrane on the posterior surface of the soft palate.

Mr. Solly records a case in St. Thomas Hospital in which the soft palate, uvula, the tonsils and pillars of the fauces were covered in many places; the base of the epiglottis being very thickly overlaid.

SECTION II.

Experiments upon the Membrane.

I.—The transudation which escaped in every case so soon as division of the trachea was effected, I have found to be serum, holding *albumen* in solution; for, following the direction of Paget, and greatly diluting it (one drachm of the transudation to four ounces of water) and adding thereto *Nitric acid*, a large albuminous deposit was thrown down.

With reference to the precise time of the appearance of the transudation in question, there may be some doubt. I had looked in vain through many treatises and essays upon Diphtheria to find among the observations of others a record of a similar fact, but was disappointed in every instance, until in Dr. Slade's treatise, p. 49, I met with the following remarks: "After very long and careful examination, it has been observed that the exudation was preceded *by a sero mucous transparent liquid, which, in some cases, is very abundant.* This liquid, once exuded, soon takes on more density and a closer adherence to the surface which secretes it, and at certain points becomes a little less transparent, assuming a yellowish tinge. These points soon run together, coalesce, and thus form a very thin pellicle, which may be regarded as the commencement of the false membrane." Here, then, we find that the fluid has been noticed by others "after very long and careful examination," and that it contains the principles of which the false membrane is afterward formed.

II.—Upon the 16th of February, the day after the third recorded autopsy had been made, at quarter before 10 o'clock P.M., I placed a portion of the membrane preserved from that examination on a slab of porcelain, and poured thereon about fifteen drops of strong *Perchloride of Iron*. This preparation had been highly recommended as a solvent of the exudation, and I was anxious to perceive its effect. In about two minutes, the diphtheritic formation to which it was applied shriveled slightly, and then appeared to harden. At twelve o'clock the same night, the hardness had increased; and on the next morning, the substance was black, dry, and perfectly tanned.

III.—A solution was next prepared of one part of pure *Nitric acid* to two of water, and a portion of exuded membrane subjected, by immersion, to its action. In twenty-six hours, it was partly decomposed and much whitened; and in thirty-six hours, the continuity was destroyed, the substance being separated into flakes.

IV.—*Muriatic acid*, diluted in the same manner, was then used, with the effect of rather hardening the membrane, but at the same time contracting its proportions considerably. In eight hours, the continuity of the substance was entirely destroyed by the addition of a little more pure acid.

V.—*Sulphuric acid*, in the same proportions as above, softened the exudation, somewhat reddened the solution, and threw down a slight precipitate, not, however, decomposing the structure.

VI.—*Benzoic acid* and *Fluoric acid* (the former diluted as above, the latter pure,) produced in a longer space of time, an effect similar to that mentioned as following the use of *Nitric acid.*

VII.—I next prepared a solution composed of equal parts of *caustic Ammonia* and water, and immersed therein a portion of the pseudo-membrane. In seven minutes, it commenced to dissolve, and in twelve minutes, no trace remained of the substance but a slight cloud within the vial. This appearance continued unchanged for thirty-six hours, and then the matter sank to the bottom of the glass on the addition of tannic acid.

VIII.—A portion of the membrane was next subjected to quite a strong solution of *caustic Potash.* For about an hour, the substance floated in the liquor, and then began to separate into particles, which gradually deposited themselves at the bottom of the glass. On the morning following, no trace of membranous formation could be observed.

IX.—A solution, composed of one part of *Hydrocyanic acid*, and two parts of water, dissolved the substance in about thirty minutes, leaving no traces excepting a whitish deposit.

X.—A preparation of *chloride of Zinc* (one I have used to preserve bodies for anatomical purposes, made by dissolving the granulated chloride in water, or one part of the disinfecting fluid of the Pharmacopæia to eighteen of water) preserved the membrane, and hardened and somewhat blackened it, making it at the same time in some degree more friable. It may be well to state here that the membrane subjected to the action of this agent was not as recent as the other portions of exudation with which the experiments were made, it having been cast off by the patient herself in the earlier part of her sickness, and had been kept in my pocket-book during the interval.

XI.—Water in which a large portion of *Phosphorus* had been immersed for the space of two years, and which was strongly impregnated with the substance, whitened the membrane, and caused a separation into flakes after twenty-eight hours exposure to it action. Lime water produced the same effect in little longer time.

It will be observed that these experiments were made with a view of ascertaining the solubility of the exudation found on the tonsils and uvula, and within the larynx of diphtheritic patients, in order, perhaps to facilitate in some instances the treatment by topical application to the local manifestation of the constitutional disease. By referring to the action of the different materials used, it will be found that *Ammonia causticum*, *Hydrocyanic acid*, *Hydrochloric acid* and *caustic Potash* were the solvents of the membrane in the shortest space of time, and that, of the remaining agents, some produced more and others less effect. It must here also be borne in mind, that the solutions to which the membrane was exposed were of such dilute character that their action was necessarily slower than if the pure substances had been employed.

I was rather gratified at the speedy action of *caustic Ammonia*, because I had prescribed the medicine frequently with benefit, but had never used it locally. Attention was particularly directed to this agent, during 1860, by the perusal of some extreme cases of Diphtheria, which had been cured by its exhibition, and which were published in the *British Journal of Homœopathy*.*

Hydrochloric acid has also been highly recommended as a local application by both Allopathic and Homœopathic writers upon Diphtheria. Some have spoken loudly of its peculiar virtues, and others have seen no effects from its application; but, be this as it may, I am certain that it possesses the power of dissolving the membranous exudation of Diphtheria.

In a strongly written article on "Diphtheria and its Treatment," Dr. Thos. P. Helsop thus writes:† "I have also applied daily, sometimes twice a day, by means of sponges, a solution of *Hydrochloric acid*, but little weaker than the dilute acid of the *London Pharmacopœia*, and have always enjoined a regular use of weaker gargles of the same acid. This, with the constant administration of stimulants, beef-tea, milk and jellies, has constituted my treatment; and I repeat here, what I have already stated in other quarters, that since I have become aware of the value of this medication, nearly ten months ago, I have not lost a single case." This gentleman, whose veracity cannot be doubted, in other

* No. LXXI, p. 159.

† Medical Times and Gazette, May 29th.

places in the same article, speaks in the most confident manner of this method of treatment, particularly his application of *Hydrochloric acid;* and if certain conclusions be correct, (and I have reached them after much thought, experiment, and study in reference to the peculiar nature and composition of the membranous exudation in Diphtheria,) the topical application of this acid or caustic ammonia may be *of some service* in the treatment, though, doubtless, it is not the all-important point to which attention should be directed, which is most certainly the virulent poison within the circulating fluid.

Much has also been said of the application of the preparations of iron—the *muriate* and *perchloride;* and alleged cures are recorded as following their use. On the recommendation of Dr. Madden, I have, in several instances used the *muriate* topically. So soon as either of these preparations touches the exuded membrane, it appears to shrivel; and if detached by the cough that supervenes, the effect may be obtained, that is, the detachment of the foreign substance. But I am convinced that, if this does not result, the exhibition of these tinctures of iron inflict absolute harm. In the first place, they tan and harden the membrane; and, in the second, they create unhealthy action in those parts of the mucous membrane which have not as yet received deposits. The experiment is a dangerous one, particularly when we consider how small a part of the true treatment of Diphtheria belongs to the absolute eradication of he membrane from the fauces. To this matter, however, allusion will be made in another portion of this work.

Section III.

The Composition of the Membrane.

Madden believes the membranous formation in Diphtheria to be distinctly albuminous; and from the observations I have made, I believe his deductions to be correct. And as recent experiments in physiology have proved that such an organization can be composed of albumen, without any fibrin, we may argue that the disease consists in an albuminous condition of the blood.*

It has been asserted by some, that false membrane must be composed of fibrin, as this is the only plastic or organizable element in the liquor sanguinis. This is contradicted by Lehmann,† who states that plastic exudations are sometimes *entirely devoid of fibrin;* and by Peasly, who argues that it is impossible that any single immediate principle can be the source of all the tissues, since all of the latter consist of several principles combined, and that albumen and fibrin *both* have the different necessary ingredients of structure associated with them. Moreover, the tissues are said to be developed and nourished by fibrin only, because all *plastic exudations* contain fibrin. If

---

* For further pathological views of the affection, the reader is referred to Section IV. This being the first step in the investigation.

† Physiological Chemistry, Vol. II., p. 290.

this were true, we might also remember that they contain albumen. This fact, taken with the assertion of Lehmann, already quoted, may prove that fibrin cannot be the *only* organizable element in the liquor sanguinis, as *albumen* must be organizable in exudations containing no fibrin. And if so in such cases, it is probably in all, for we find no exudation not containing *albumen*. These ideas are somewhat contradicted by Gluge,* who writes, "The organization of fibrin into fibres and *cells* is a matter of direct observation." We are all aware that simple coagulation of fibrin produces fibres; but there is no proof, as yet, that cells are the product of that substance, for, in his chapter on Cytology, Peasly writes,† "The cell wall is formed of simple membrane, and of course is an *albuminous* compound, *but is not fibrin;*" p. 115, "The fluid contained in the cells is almost invariably transparent, or nearly so: in the blood corpuscles, however, it is of a bright red color: in chemical composition, it varies extremely, *being usually an albuminous compound*—in part at least;" p. 117, "The membranous wall of the nuclei is an *albuminous compound certainly*, and probably but little, if at all, different from the younger cell membrane." And further, on p. 157, he writes, "they [the cells] are probably *never* developed from fibrin, but from *albumen* rather, fibrin never rising to a higher organization than mere simple fibre." And still, on the same subject, he writes, in speaking of false membrane, "It

---

* Pathological Histology, p. 50.

† Histology, p. 114.

must therefore be something else that is converted into cells and tissues, and we can assign no other element than *albumen.* In respect, therefore, to the tissues, *albumen,* and not fibrin, *is the plastic element* of the blood plasma."

That the membrane is albuminous may be verified—

1st, by the albuminous precipitate resulting from the addition of *Nitric acid* to the transudation which had been preserved from the last autopsy.

2d, by the same deposit being thrown down by tannic acid.

3d, by coagulation upon the application of heat.

4th, by the solution of the foreign substance in caustic alkalies.

5th, *perhaps* by the presence of the exudation within *the right heart.*

6th, the membrane found within the right heart was not fibrinous. Fibrin from the veins is rather different in formation from the same substance taken from arterial blood; and according to Draper,* the former may be dissolved in a warm solution of nitrate of potash, while the latter cannot. A portion of the cardiac exudation was subjected to this test, without the slightest effect being produced, while caustic ammonia immediately dissolved it.

7th, fibrin is dissolved by cold, concentrated muriatic acid, and if kept at a cool temperature for twenty-four hours, the solution acquires a

---

* Medical Chemistry, p. 390.

dark indigo-blue color. Albumen, similarly heated, acquires a violet hue.* Many portions of Diphtheritic exudation were submitted to this test, under varying circumstances, and the *violet hue was always* developed.

SECTION IV.

Deductions.

From all these circumstances, I believe that Diphtheria is certainly a malignant blood disease. The zymotic action greatly affecting the nervous centres, prevents the conversion of albumen into fibrin, and the virus still being carried to those localities whereon it appears to have the most especial action, causes, in the majority of instances, the membranous deposit to appear in those parts of the human system. As the fibrin in the blood is obtained in part from the chyle and lymph, and in *all three* of these fluids comes from their albumen—as we are aware that certain poisons, those of malignant typhus and glanders, for instance, prevent the coagulation of the blood by the *destruction of the fibrin*, so I believe, the diphtheritic poison prevents by its action the conversion of *albumen* into fibrin; and hence the nature of the deposit, which, as has been remarked, *can of itself* become organized from albumen alone. But there is another circumstance that forced itself upon my mind while thinking of the pecular endocardial deposit

* Todd & Bowman, Physiology, p. 55.

found in the last autopsy. Why was the pseudo-membrane only within the *right heart*, and following the direct course of the *venous* circulation? For a time, this appearance was not easily explained; but, on reference to works upon this subject, I found an idea of Lehmann's, "That fibrin is produced by the oxidation of albumen in the aeration of the blood." Now, if this be true, more light is thrown upon the albuminous character of the deposit. When we recollect that, in making the examinations, we have found a great deposit of false membrane on *the anterior face of the epiglottis;* that in all, more or less, the rima-glottidis was much contracted by the shutting down of its valve and by tumefaction; that false membrane blocked up the air passages, and that the lungs were in a state of collapse; necessarily, there must be but a small amount of oxygen taken into the lungs to create the transformation of albumen into fibrin, and consequently the circulating fluid, overloaded with this substance, deposited an albuminous compound at that part of the body where the accumulated stream was greatest, and where it had arrived overcharged with the material which, in the lungs, was to be changed into fibrin for the repair of the tissues.

These ideas were also somewhat confirmed by the fact that *fibrinous deposits* are always, or in far the greater majority of instances, observed in the *left heart.* Speaking of this fact, and at the same time alluding to the truth that formations may occur within the central organ of the circulation *without* *inflammation* (and there was no trace of such action in the heart I examined), Professor Simon thus writes:* "If they are inflammatory exudations, why should they evince so decided a preference to the LEFT heart? Both sides of the heart, and all points of each cavity, are equally exposed to the causes of inflammation; the coronary arteries supply both ventricles of the heart indifferently; and we well know that acute pericarditis pays no respect to the grooves and septum of the heart. * * * * I believe that the origin of these vegetations is directly humoral; that they arise as a *fibrinous* precipitation from an overchaged solution (observe, in *the left heart*), the valves, &c., incrusting themselves with fibrin, as a stick in certain streams coats itself with a calcareous envelope." * * * * "You will observe that this theory involves the supposition *that arterial blood is more prone than venous blood to precipitate its fibrin.*"

The Professor then goes on to state some very conclusive experiments with reference to this matter. He passed a single thread, by means of a very fine needle, transversely through the artery and vein of a dog, leaving it there that it might cut the stream. This was done repeatedly, sometimes with the femoral vessels, sometimes with the carotid and jugular, and always with uniform results—the thread always receiving a *fibrinous* deposit within the artery, and no incrustation on that portion passing through the vein.

Now, recollecting these facts—1st, that we have

* General Pathology, p. 47.

found an *albuminous* deposit in the *right heart*, following the direct course of the venous circulation; 2d, that *fibrinous* deposits are most generally discovered in the *left heart;* 3d, that, from actual experiment, the vital fluid in the arteries uniformly contains and deposits *fibrin;* 4th, that Lehmann has asserted the fact that the aeration of blood within the lungs converts albumen into fibrin; 5th, that, so far as our observations have gone, the greatest exudations in Diphtheria are noticed in such positions as effectually impede the ingress of atmospheric air to the lungs; 6th, that we know the blood poisons of certain diseases likewise prevent the transformation of albumen into fibrin; and, 7th, that the exudations themselves, in Diphtheria, are conceded to be distinctly albuminous—may we not arrive at the conclusion that the diphtheritic poison, first within the blood, prevents the necessary transformation of albumen into fibrin? that the false membrane is thrown off in localities, which (if Lehmann's theory be correct, and which Simon's experiments, already detailed, appear to prove,) still further prevents this necessary change, wherefore the tissues not being supplied with their pabulum, waste from imperfect nutrition? and that excessive prostration is the result—a prostration so rapid and excessive that life is proof against it, in some instances, but a few hours?

There are also other circumstances that tend strongly to force upon my mind the correctness of the theory in reference to the albuminous nature, not only of the membrane, but of the blood of diphtheritic patients.

One of the strongest of which is the albuminuria, which is generally present to a greater or lesser degree in every case.

SECTION V.

Albuminuria.

By the term Albuminuria, is understood a peculiar condition of the urine; it containing albumen in greater or less quantities. With many physicians this word is used as synonymous with a peculiar abnormal condition of the kidneys, termed Morbus Brightii, or Bright's disease, or with certain puerperal states in which albumen is found in the renal secretion. In fact, several treatises by very eminent authorities, bearing the title of *Albuminuria*,* are nothing more than essays on the disease of the kidneys already mentioned, or of the enclampsia of child-bed. This confusion is the less pardonable, because there are many disorders to which the body is subject, that have albuminous urine either as a concomitant or a sequel. Dr. Bedford† quotes the following from Edward Robin:‡ "The urine becomes albuminous in croup, in ascites and in cases of capillary bronchitis with emphysema accompanied by dyspnœa. In pulmonary phthisis, in gestation where sufficiently advanced to occasion an habitual congestion of the kidneys

* Vide such an article in 1st Vol. of the Transactions of the New York Academy of Medicine.

† Principles and Practice of Obstet., p. 511.

‡ Ed. Robin, London Lancet, Jan. 24th, 1852, p. 96.

in cyanosis, in diabetes, etc. etc." He then goes on to remark that experiments of Bareswil, Cl. Bernard, Brown-Sequard and Dr. Hammond, all go to prove that albumen may exist in the urine without any structural change in the kidney, or *without* producing any symptoms of anæmia.

The question then arises, What are the causes of albumen being noted in the urinary secretion of those suffering from Diphtheria. In the first place, we are all now well aware of the high position that albumen bears in the process of digestion; and in fact, as has been mentioned already, the fibrin in the blood, chyle and lymph, first comes from their albumen; or, according to Lehmann,* who thus speaks: "After what has been said of the occurrence of albumen, it seems scarcely necessary to adduce any further proof of its utility in *forming* and *renovating* the nitrogenous tissues of the animal body. In fact, *the whole theory of nutrition* rests upon this postulate." Now, we know very well that there are certain zymotic diseases that prevent the transformation of albumen into fibrin, and although we agree in a measure with the views expressed by Dr. Fletcher,† in reference to the revival of humoral pathology, still we must give due credit to the more recent investigations in pathological science, which are expressed by the editors of the said volume in a foot-note of considerable length. Diphtheria is most certainly one of these disorders, and the zymotic process going on in the system

---

* Physiological Chemistry, Vol. I, p. 309.

† General Pathology, pp. 84, 85.

does not allow the albumen to be transformed into the renovating tissues, and consequently the blood is loaded with the compound. Again, we have already adverted to the fact, that Lehmann has proved, by direct experiment, that proper oxidation of the blood is necessary to transform albumen into fibrin. To this he alludes again in the following: *"No one can doubt that the albuminous substances in the blood undergo a gradual oxidation, *before they can be employed in* the formation or renovation of the tissues," etc. Now, in very many cases of Diphtheria, we are aware that the membrane is so deposited as to prevent the free ingress of air to the lungs, which would be but another reason for supposing the blood to be unable, through this channel, to throw off its albumen; therefore, we may perceive why the kidneys, the great emunctories of the system, should be called upon to assist in a measure, at least, in depriving the system of that albumen with which the circulating fluid is overcharged.

Albuminuria may also be explained by the action of the diphtheritic virus upon the ganglionic system of nerves supplying the kidneys. The well known action of this peculiar poison upon the nervous system, as evinced by both the symptoms and more particularly by the sequelæ of the disease, would lead certainly to the belief that the renal nerves could not be exempt from the action of the virus.

A general nervous condition may also so disarrange the system as to give rise to what Dr.

* Lehmann's Physiological Chemistry, Vol. II, p. 356.

Clark terms, a passive congestion of the kidney. He says on this point: "The consequence of this congestion is, to reduce the kidney to a condition in which it can no longer separate the urea from the blood in the usual quantity of urea.

Therefore, it appears that we may find, without looking further into the matter, quite sufficient reasons for the presence of albumen in the urine of those persons affected with Diphtheria, when we understand the true pathology of the disease. 1st. Diphtheria is a *zymotic* disease, the virus changing the character of the blood, and that very mutation tending to overload the circulating fluid with *albumen.* 2d. The action of the poison on the nerves of the kidneys, as well as the whole nervous system, as has been proven, will produce the appearance of albumen in the urine. So far, then, for the appearance of albumen *without* structural change. When such organic disease exists, then there need be no difficulty in explaining the appearance presented in the urine. The only important question then arising being, Does the structural change belong to the Diphtheria, or was it existing prior to the invasion of the diphtheritic attack. I am inclined to believe that in by far the greater majority of cases of Diphtheria, no such structural renal disease, exists, and in those few post-mortem examinations that have shown an altered kidney, the disorder had been present before the patient had been attacked with Diphtheria, or at least a latent renal disease had only been aroused into action by the general poisoning of the systen by the diphtheritic virus.

Greenhow makes a difference between Diphtheria and scarlet fever—by the early appearance of albuminuria in the former and its later development in the latter.

Casts of the tubuli uriniferi have been seen in the urine; but I have often known great albuminous deposit to be present, and not uriniferous casts. The same fact is mentioned by Drs. Helsop and Haughton, of England. On this subject, Greenhow says: "The presence of albumen in the urine must always be regarded as a serious circumstance in Diphtheria; and of course, more so, if the albumen be in large quantity. But neither is its presence an absolutely fatal symptom, nor does it always coincide with great severity in the other symptoms." In the second report of the Medical Officer of the Privy Council, Dr. Sanderson says, that albumen was found in the urine in all cases except one in which it was sought for. Dr. Webb found it in every case in which he examined the urine. At Crowle, albumen was frequently found in the urine; but in some severe and fatal cases, it could not be discovered.

It must be confessed, however, that the subject is, as yet involved in much obscurity, and demands much enterprise, experiment and experience to substantiate the true pathology of the affection.

Section VI.

Other Pathological Views.

The connection of Diphtheria with a parasitic fungus, mentioned by writers on the subject, deserves to be noticed. From the observations of many, not much reliance can be placed in the appearance of the oidium albicans in the diphtheritic exudations. For a confirmation of this assertion, we may refer to a note to Dr. Preston's article on Diphtheria, published in the *United States Journal of Homœopathy;* and to the experience of Dr. Wilks,* who states, that, in the cases that had passed under his own observation, the fungus was always present, and that at first he was disposed to believe this peculiar growth constituted the true character of the malady. He says also, "My attention being directed to this matter, I took the opportunity to examine the films which occasionally form on the mouths of those sick with various diseases, and upon submitting them to a microscopic test, felt some surprise in witnessing in all, fungous growth which I have not been able to distinguish from that of Diphtheria." He mentions the case of a woman who had died under his care with acute cerebral and spinal meningitis, upon examining the pharynx after death, a pellicle was found composed of the parasitic growth. Several other instances are recorded in which the same

* Medical Times and Gazette, p. 354.

growth was detected, when there was no diphtheritic disease, properly so called; and Greenhow remarks, "Low forms of cryptogamic plants are occasionally found on the exudation, which gave rise to the belief that the disease is of parasitic origin. This opinion is disproved by the facts, that on the one hand, the supposed parasite is not invariably present in Diphtheria, and on the other, that it is frequently found on unhealthy mucous surfaces, which are not of a diphtheritic nature."

There have been other ideas suggested by post-mortem examinations as to the pathology of Diphtheria; some have supposed its main centre to be in the kidneys, and that from these organs the origin of the disorder may be traced.

Dr. Gull suggests, the spinal cord as the original seat of the disease, and adduces, from this, an explanation of the paralytic symptoms which are noticed at a late stage of the disease, or as sequelæ of the affection.

CHAPTER VII.—TREATMENT.

Some members of our school have been very successful in the treatment of Diphtheria, managing hundreds of cases without a single death, while others have not been as fortunate. I belong to the latter class, and have had under my care some cases that proceeded from bad to worse without a single favorable symptom, rushing onward unchecked by every means that were used to arrest the progress of the disorder, and terminating fatally in from three to seven or fourteen days.

Before proceeding to state the internal medicines for Diphtheria, it may not be amiss to say a word in reference to topical applications; and to offer a few remarks upon the methods of examining the fauces.

Section I.

Examination of the Mouth, &c.

In adults, it is not generally a difficult matter to obtain a view of the inside of the buccal cavity, because they readily can understand the necessity for such examination; for their own welfare they do as they are bidden, and permit the spoon handle, or other instrument for depressing the tongue, to be inserted within the mouth; but in certain cases of disease, even the separation of the jaws is effected with much pain, and when inflammatory action has stiffened and swollen the tongue, and the muscles at its base, quite severe suffering is often engendered by the requisite examination of the parts. In such instances the patient should be made to sit facing as strong light as possible, and if the disease prevents wide separation of the jaws, a small mirror may be used to throw either reflected light from a candle, or lamp, held by an assistant, or the rays of the sun, within the mouth; then, by inserting the handle of a spoon or the ordinary tongue depressor—the shape and size of which are familiar to all—as far back as possible, pressure should be made downwards, slight at first, but gradually and steadily increasing, until the spasm of the muscles at the base of the tongue is overcome, and a satisfactory view of the parts in question obtained. This method will succeed in the majority of instances, when the patient has arrived at an age sufficient to comprehend the necessity of the operation; but in young children, there is not one of the minor duties of the physician which requires so much patience, and which is often so unsuccessful as the simple examination of the fauces.

There is danger of children being thrown into convulsions by the force actually required to effect an opening between the tightly clenched teeth, and I have known relapses to occur from the same cause. The child, on such occasions, sets its teeth firmly together, and persuasion, entreaties, bribes, punishment, or pain, are alike unavailing. In such instances, the better plan, after patient and gentle entreaty has been tried in vain, is to take the nostrils firmly between the forefinger and thumb of the left hand, and holding the depressor (whichever kind be selected) in the right hand, patiently wait for an inspiration; the ingress of air by the nostrils being prevented, the child will slightly gasp, when, with a rapid and dexterous movement, the instrument is gotten partly into the mouth; but at this period the teeth again are firmly closed upon the depressor, and a little more patience is required. It is not well either to wrench the instrument, or to try to prize open the mouth by force—teeth are broken and gums lacerated by such proceeding; the better method is to hold the nose, as before, and forcibly blow into the mouth through the slight aperture on either side of the spoon handle; another gasp is the result, and by quickly slipping back the instrument to the fauces, a choking sensation is produced; the child gags, the curtain of the soft palate is raised, and the whole isthmus of the fauces brought to view. Another method, if the child will listen to reason, is to have the mouth open; request the patient to project the tongue outward as far as possible, and to say loudly, and prolonged—Ah! h-h-h! This pronunciation depresses the base of the tongue and elevates the soft palate, and a good view of the parts is obtained.

For the better removal of the diphtheritic exudation, or, indeed, in certain surgical operations, it is necessary that a variety of speculum be used, which will depress the tongue and keep the jaws asunder, thus allowing the surgeon free use of both hands, and preventing interruption of the operation by closure of the teeth. One of the best instruments for this purpose is constructed by Luer, of Paris, and other cutlers. It is formed of a plate of German silver, bent into a circle, with eyelet holes on the one side of its extremity, and a button on the other, in order that it may be adapted to the capacity of different mouths, and having at its base, projecting at right angles, a horizontal tongue piece, permanently attached.

When this instrument is inserted between tne jaws, their closure is prevented, while the tongue is kept down, and out of the way of the operator. It is made of two sizes, for children and adults; each, however, can be lessened or increased in circumference.

The instrument is used frequently by M. Rayer, at La Charite, Paris, and was by him, I believe, introduced to the notice of the profession. Charriere has also constructed a mouth speculum on the principle of his well-known speculum vaginæ. It is, however, considerably more expensive than the above, but has the advantage of being either enlarged or diminished in size to suit all ages.

Dr. J. Smith* introduces a speculum to be employed during operations upon the mouth—the patient being under anæsthetic influence.

The journal says, though it is very simple, yet it must be considered a very important addition to surgical appliances, for every one experienced in these operations, knows how often he has been inconvenienced for the want of an instrument which will keep the mouth open, and, at the same time, prevent no impediment to the admission of air, or to the free course of the operation. For a description and a plate of this instrument, the reader is referred to Rankin's abstract, for 1849, page 248.

---

* Edinburgh Monthly Journal, April, 1854.

SECTION II.

Topical Applications.

When Diphtheria was first noticed, a great many articles were thrust upon the notice of the profession and the public as certain specifics. These have fallen generally into disrepute among the members of the Homœopathic school, as the true character of the disease is better understood. So far as my own experience goes, I believe topical applications are not serviceable, and I have tried many—such as *Muriatic acid*, *Muriated tincture of Iron*, *Perchloride of Iron*, *Alum*, *Tannin*, *Yeast*, *Kali-chlor*, and others. I never now employ any thing, saving perhaps a solution of *Muriatic acid* and water, directing all my attention to the proper selection of the medicine to arrest the constitutional disease. If there is much swelling and rigidity of the muscles and glands, the fat of pork or bacon should be applied, warm, to the outside of the throat, and, so far as topical applications are concerned, this is all that I can recommend. I am convinced, from considerable experience, that since I have not resorted to any chemical re-agents, that my patients have gotten along better than when they were applied.

We believe the disease to be one of the blood; to be a constitutional affection, and, therefore, so far as *curative* agencies are concerned, topical applications are of no value; there may be, however, instances in which, from the symptoms, we believe the larynx not involved, and suffocation, from the presence of the exudation within the fauces, may be imminent; in such cases, as a means of palliation, or to gain time for the action of medicines internally exhibited, a topical application may be recommended.

Some Allœopathic authorities do not sanction the use of escharotics in malignant Diphtheria—and wisely so—the cause remaining unabated, the effect, or the production of the false membrane will continue, additional inflammatory action will certainly supervene, and the patient's sufferings will be increased; while the nervous system may also be seriously affected by the excitement produced by operations.

However, as many practitioners are in favor of these adjuvants, and in deference to the position occupied in our school by those who recommend them, it is proper that such should be herein enumerated.

Dr. Madden at first employed the *muriate of Iron* and *Glycerine*. He directs, once every twelve hours, the fauces to be painted with the pure tincture of the *muriate of Iron*, and four times, daily, with *Glycerine;* but from the preface to Dr. Morgan's Essay on Diphtheria, it appears that he (Dr. Madden) has rather preferred of late the *Muriatic acid.** Dr. Suss Hahnemann reports a case in which he used the preparation of iron and glycerine with

* British Journal of Homœopathy, Vol. XVII, p. 232.

great advantage. Mr. Gelston* speaks as follows: "Sydenham recommended *Sulph. acid*, mixed with honey, as a detergent. Bearing in mind that the local affection of the throat is an acrid exudation, means calculated to modify its nature and to arrest its propagation, should not be overlooked. *Alum, sulphate of Copper or Zinc*, separately, or in combination with tincture of myrrh, catechu, or the like, in the form of a gargle, may be judiciously employed." Drs. Black and Smith recommend *nitrate of Silver* topically.

Dr. Morgan and others, *Hydrochloric acid*. It would be almost an endless task to run over the great number of topical medicines which have been recommended by Allœopathic authors—all kinds of substances have been highly recommended, viz: *Spirits of Turpentine; Alum*, in solution or powder; *Tannin, oil Pennyroyal, Iodine, Tar*, &c., &c.

To give the reader a sample of the many "*unfailing*" remedies which have been recommended by Allœopathic authors, and also to point out their treatment of the disease—which certainly is a point of interest and curiosity—and, perhaps, as a suggestion for the study of the symptoms of the *Actea Racemosa*, the following quotation from a Boston journal is inserted:

"I doubt not the public will kindly receive any suggestions which may contribute to a more successful treatment of this modern scourge; and therefore venture to give publicity to the treatment

* British Journal of Homœopathy, July 1st, 1861, p. 418.

used by myself *with unfailing success.* The remedy on which I chiefly depend is the Actea Racemosa, or Black Snakeroot, which is used both locally as a gargle, and taken internally. As a gargle, one tea-spoonful of the tincture is added to two table-spoonsful of water, and gargled *every hour* for twenty-four hours, or till the progress of the disease is arrested; after which the intervals may be extended to an hour and a half, or more, as the symptoms may justify. In connection with the use of the gargle, or separately, the adult patient should take internally to the amount of two or three tea-spoonsful of the tincture in the course of twenty-four hours.

"In addition to the foregoing, I give ten drops of the muriated tincture of iron three times in the twenty-four hours, and a powder of three to five grains of the chlorate of potash in the interval. Under this treatment, a very decided improvement takes place within the first twenty-four hours, the ash-colored membrane disappears *usually within two days*, and the patient overcomes the malignant tendency of the disease."

Many physicians of the old school employ insufflations of *Alum* combined with *Tannic acid*, as recommended by Trousseau; indeed, some rely upon this as the only topical application.* Solutions of *Potassæ chloras*, acidulated with *Hydrochloric acid*, have also been highly lauded.

There can be no surer evidence of the intracta-

---

* Vide American Medical Times, 1862, p. 234.

bility of a disease than the recommendation of a hundred "*sure cures.*" Every body knows a certain remedy for intermittent fever and rheumatism, and, notwithstanding, these disorders still trouble the most scientific and well-read physicians, in the application of their remedies.

The best of all the extraneous means is a solution composed of two parts of *Muriatic acid* to one of water, applied with a soft sponge over the fauces and those parts which appear covered with the exudation, and this repeated twice or thrice in the twenty-four hours: such application may be necessary in cases wherein the false membrane, by its quantity, appears to be pressing down the epiglottis and threatening suffocation. The great difficulty, however, is the act of applying the solution to the patient, particularly in children. Every one who has attempted this, will agree with me on this point.

There is, however, one other topical application, which has lately been recommended, which deserves some attention, and that is a solution of *chlorinated Soda.* The preparation known as Beaufoy's is said to be the best; and, according to Dr. Wm. Budd, senior physician to the Bristol Royal Infirmary,* who has tried all the preparations in vogue, it is superior to all others. He thus writes:

"In all the cases in which I have hitherto tried it—amounting now to fifteen—the local disease has begun to decline from the moment of its first application. An immediate subsidence of swelling of

* Vide British Medical Journal, June, 1861, p. 575; or, Braithwaite's Retrospect, Part XLIV, p. 56.

the lymphatics, in the neighborhood of the disease, has, in particular, always followed its use—a fact from which the inference seems pretty clear, that this agent may do much to prevent that secondary poisoning of the system by the absorption of putrescent matters from the throat, which, in many cases, has the chief hand in giving a malignant turn to the malady.

"On the other hand, its employment is attended by little or no pain: it causes no inflammation, and it leads to none of those breaches of surface which are inseparable from the repeated use of powerful escharotics, and which, when once produced, often make convalescence so painful and protracted.

"Lastly—and this alone is a consideration of the highest importance—by exercising a local disinfection in the very focus of the diphtheritic virus, there is reason to suppose that this preparation greatly lessens the contagious power of the malady."

The solution is applied with a full-bodied camel's hair pencil, and is directed to be used three or four times daily.

SECTION III.

Internal Medicines.

Before alluding to those remedial agents, which have been used in the treatment of Diphtheria, it is well to remark, that, as yet we are without a *true specific* for the disease, *after it has invaded the larynx and trachea*—such complication being evinced by the croupy cough. This observation is verified by most physicians of both schools, who have been close observers of the phenomena of Diphtheria.

David Thomas, Esq.,* thus writes: "Of 485 cases that came under my own observation, the instances in which the air-passages became involved in the disease, amounted to 15; and of this number 11 died—the greater number within a few hours after the croupy breathing began. * * * * I kept accurate notes of 125 of the most severe cases, including all the deaths, with the following results: Males 55—deaths, 9; females, 70—deaths, 4. The deaths, with two exceptions, *were all from affections of the air-passages.*"

That the appropriate treatment, in the earlier stages of the disease, arrests the membranous formation within the pharynx and fauces, is very certain; but, if the case is not seen until the exudation has proceeded to the larynx and trachea, there is no medicine, as far as my own observation extends, upon which much reliance can be placed.

Those remedial agents which have been found most efficacious, are not numerous, and the curative action of each has been variously estimated by different writers upon Diphtheria.

Some years since, while reading a cast-away number of the *London Lancet*, I was struck by the account of an accidental poisoning by *tinct. Cantharides*, which a traveler had taken, mistaking it for some

* British Medical Journal, 1859.

other medicinal substance. The symptoms there recorded, were salivation, intense soreness of the mouth and throat, suffocating breathing, &c. Since then, I have employed the medicine successfully in various cases of stomatitis.

Bretonneau, in his treatise upon Diphtheria, has experimented with the drug, and has found no substance capable of producing similar effects.

He says,* "The action of the oil of cantharides, when applied to the surface of the tongue and lips, is almost instantaneous. In less than thirty minutes, the epidermis shrivels, and becomes raised and detached. It is soon re-placed by a concrete pellicle, at first thin and semi-transparent, which speedily becomes more opaque and thicker. Like the diphtheritic exudation, this membrane, which is at first slightly adherent, is detached and reproduced with great readiness. Within a period of six or seven days, it may be several times renewed."

Dr. Slade remarks, that from these facts M. Bretonneau concludes, that the *membrane of Cantharides is identical with that of Diphtheria.*

Dr. Sanderson† has tried the effect of injecting a solution of *Cantharides*, in olive oil, into the air-passages of dogs, and found that, two hours after the application, the mucous surface of the larynx was scattered over with patches scarce perceptibly redder than the surrounding membrane; and that the structure was covered co-extensively with

---

* Vide Fiske Fund Prize Essay, p. 51; also, Greenhow, p. 117.

† British and Foreign Med. Chirg. Review, January, 1860, pp. 181–9.

these patches with a gelatinous covering of tolerably firm concretion, differing from that of Diphtheria only in its greater transparency.

From these facts, it would appear that *Cantharides* should always be considered in the selection of the medicines for Diphtheria, as we find it capable of producing, within the larynx and trachea, a true pseudo-membrane, which is identical in appearance and formation with that found in Diphtheria.

Its effects are often surprising.

Some time since, I was sent for to see a young man who had been unwell for some days, and had complained of sore throat; upon examining the fauces, I found slight spots of membranous formation, and diagnosed the disease as diphtheritic sore throat; the prescription was *Acon.* and *Merc. prot.*, every two hours—the former in solution, the latter in trituration. In four days, he was convalescent, and imprudently resumed his labor. On the third day thereafter, I was summoned again, and found the tonsils covered—the left one entirely, the right one partially, with diphtheritic formation; there was great prostration, complete anorexia, and labored respiration; for two days, the symptoms increased steadily, and I could foresee nothing but a fatal termination. During this period, the usual medicines for Diphtheria were administered, but without effect. At this juncture, I prescribed *Cantharides*, 2d dil., ten drops in four ounces of water, a dessert-spoonful to be given every two hours. The improvement was evident upon the next visit; and on the second day after, I lifted from both tonsils large and very thick membranes. On the fourth day, violent itching of the whole surface of the body appeared, and existed to such an extent that the patient at times was rendered almost delirious. *Sulphur* was then exhibited, and recovery progressed; but to this day the voice is nasal, fluids return by the nostrils, and impaired vision exists at times to such a degree that the usual business cannot be transacted.

I have also, in several instances, noted the beneficent action of *Cantharides*, in almost hopeless cases of the disease.

There is another medicine to which attention should be directed, and that is *caustic Ammonia.*

In the "Elements of a New Materia Medica," in the *North American Journal of Homœopathy*, the following case, from *Christison on Poisons*, is well worthy of remark:

"A medical man, liable to epilepsy, was found in a fit by his servant, who tried to arouse him by holding to his nose a handkerchief dipped in ammonia. On recovering his senses, he complained of burning pains in the mouth down to the stomach, great difficulty in swallowing, difficult breathing, hard cough, copious expectoration, profuse mucous discharge from the nostrils, and excoriation of the tongue. The bronchitis increased steadily, and carried him off in three days.

"*Post-mortem appearances.*—The nostrils were blocked up with an *albuminous false membrane;* the whole mucous coat of the larynx, trachea, bronchi, and even some of the bronchial ramifications, were mottled with patches of *lymph.* Hence it seems to produce a true *croupous inflammation.* The gullet and stomach showed red streaks here and there; and there was a black eschar on the tongue, and another on the lower lip."

In the case that has been recorded at length in the preceeding pages, it will be observed that *Ammonium caust.* was the first medicine that appeared to exercise a beneficial action upon the disease. Others have also noted the action of the drug. Dr. Smith of Oldham,* who probably was led to the selection of the medicine in question, by the quotation from Christison, which he appends to the record of his case, has observed the most conclusive evidence of the action of *caustic Ammonia.* A portion of the records of a case "of malignant Diphtheria" reads thus:

"10.30 P. M. Evidently worse. I now lost all hopes of saving him. I left a mixture of *Nitric acid* A, ordering a little to be given to him every few minutes, and having to go some distance to a labor, I left in the care of his father *Ammonia caust.* 1, with instructions that if no change for the better was shortly observed, he was to substitute the *Ammonia* for the *Nitric acid.*

2.40 A. M., October 31st. Upon visiting my patient at this hour, I was most agreeably surprised to find him better, opening his eyes when I addressed him, breathing freer, and altogether relieved. Upon inquiry, I was informed that, no improvement being perceived by half-past eleven,

---

* British Journal of Homœopathy, LXXI, p. 159.

his father had given him the *Amm. caust.* as directed; this was followed shortly afterwards by his 'vomiting some tough stringy phlegm,' since which he had been gradually improving."

This case recovered rapidly and steadily. In describing a second case, the same author writes:

"The tonsils were enlarged—one more especially, but which I do not remember—with numerous aphthous looking ulcerations upon them. I gave her a powder of *Arsen.*, 3, to be mixed in water, and a spoonful to be taken at first every two hours, afterwards every four hours. She had previously been taking some *Belladonna* pilules. The next morning, her son came to say she was much worse, and could scarcely swallow. I sent her *Merc. iod.*, 1, to be taken every two hours, and one drachm of *chlorate of Potash*, to be dissolved in a pint of water, and drank frequently. The following morning, I was again visited by the son, with the information that his mother seemed better for a few hours, after taking the last medicine, but was now as bad, or worse, than ever. I now gave him a mixture of *Amm. caust.*, six drops, in *aqua* ℥ viij, a desert-spoonful to be taken every two hours. I heard nothing more of the case until last evening, when the woman called with her husband at my house, whilst I was out, and left word that 'she had never had anything to do her so much good in her life; that every spoonful seemed to give her new life, and she felt better then than for a long period.'"

To illustrate the treatment of the disease, I

would here introduce, as concisely as possible, the general indications and manner of administration of those medicines, which an actual experience of a number of years has taught as being most effective in the disease, after which the therapeutical views of others shall receive the attention they deserve.

We have every reason to believe, in the present state of our knowledge, that the use of our hitherto greatly renowned febrifuge, must give place, in Diphtheria, at least in this climate, to another agent which appears to possess much more power over the disease. In *Gelseminum* we find this agent, and, from the experience of all those who have administered it in the disorder, its value cannot be well over-estimated.

In that class of disorders in which the *vital forces* are suddenly and fearfully prostrated; when the system needs a constant and rapid stimulation, *Gelseminum* will ultimately supersede the use of *Aconite.* There are, however, some indications for its use, which it is well to remember.

It is especially applicable in those cases, in the commencement of the disease, where the fever is excessively high, with throbbing headache, aching in the bones, difficult deglutition, and some tendency to sleep. It must then be prescribed as follows, and in sufficient doses to make a rapid impression on the system:

℞ Gelsemini, tinct., gtt. xv.
(**A**) Aquæ font, - - ℥ iv.
M. S a tablespoonful every hour; to be

continued until more or less perspiration manifests itself.

I can state here, on positive authority, that severe, and, to all appearances, malignant cases of Diphtheria, after large patches of membrane had formed upon the fauces, have been cut short by the timely exhibition of this most powerful medicine.

Those who desire to administer Aconite in the earlier stages of Diphtheria, should do so in alternation with A, as follows:

℞ Aconiti, 1st dil., - gtt. x
(**B**) Aquæ font, - - ℥ iv

When the patient begins to complain of sore throat, with flushed face, give in alternation with A,

℞ Bella., 2d, - - gtt. vj.
(**C**) Aquæ font, - - ℥ ij.

S, every hour during the day, a tablespoonful.

When the appearance presented in the throat, is that of the primary formation of membrane, as exhibited by a somewhat shining appearance,

℞ Cantharis, tinct., gtt. x
(**D**) Aquæ, - - - ℥ j

S six drops, in a teaspoonful of water, every hour, in alternation with B.

If, during this stage, hemorrhage from the nostrils should supervene, give,

℞ Crocus sat., 1st dil., gtt. x
(**E**) Aquæ font, - - ℥ iv
vel.
℞ Hamamelis virg., tinct., gtt. v
(**F**) Aquæ font, - - ℥ ij

A teaspoonful, every 15 minutes, for an hour, then resume other treatment for two hours, and again administer from E and F as the symptoms require. If this does not suffice, and the hemorrhage continue; continue the medicines for the disease, and plug the nostrils with a solution of—

℞ Liquor Ferri, per-sulph, gtt. x
(G) Aquæ font, - - ℥ ij
M. ft. in sol.

When the glands of the neck commence to swell, give, in alternation with D—

(H) ℞ Merc. prot., ij trit., pulv. No. x
A powder every two hours.

When the fœtor begins to manifest itself—

℞ Kali-chlor., pura, grs. x
(I) Aquæ font, - - ℥ ij

A teaspoonful every hour, for three hours, and the fourth hour a tablespoonful from D, and so continue.

When the membrane begins to assume a darkish hue, and is rather more opaque—

℞ Kali-bichromat., 1st, grs. v
(K) Aquæ, - - - ℥ vj
A teaspoonful every two hours.

In some children, this may produce nausea and vomiting. If so, it must be diluted. During this stage, one of the following must be given:

℞ Arsen. alb., ij trit., grs. x
(L) Aquæ, - - - ℥ ij
vel.
℞ Ars. jodat., ij trit., grs. x
(M) Aquæ, - - - ℥ ij

vel.

Particularly for puffiness about the eyes and a peculiar pallor of the skin—

℞ Apis mel., tinct., gtt. xx
(N) Aquæ, - - - ℥ vj

vel.

(O) ℞ China, tinct., - - fl℥ss
S five drops every hour.

vel.

℞ Ferri pyro-phosph., grs. xv
(P) Aquæ font, - - ℥ iv

During all this treatment, the patient is to be rubbed, at least once in three hours, with whisky and salt, and brandy and water with beef essence exhibited as often as possible.

It very frequently happens, in severe cases of Diphtheria, that for the first hours after the administration of a medicine, an evident beneficial action results, the case progressing favorably—and then appearing stationary. This is particularly applicable to the *chlorate of Potash.* When such is the case, other medicines must be substituted. This stage of prostration may also be combatted with—

℞ Acidi hydrochlor., 1st dil., gtt. x
(Q) Aquæ font, - - - ℥ ij
S a teaspoonful every two hours.

When the disorder does not yield to disease, or rather when the *constitutional disturbance* appears to increase, and the local manifestations (as evinced by the disappearance of the membrane from the fauces) diminish, the practitioner *must be upon his guard—collapse, rapid* and fatal may terminate the life of the patient in six or eight hours. At this critical stage, the medicines, besides the Arsenicals, are—

℞ Argent. nit., ij trit., grs. x
(**R**) Sacch. lac., - - ʒ ij
M. et fet in pulv. No. X. S a powder every hour.

vel.

℞ Cupri sulph., ij trit., grs. xv
(**S**) Sach. lac., - - ʒ ij
M et ft. in pulv. No. X. S a powder every hour.

In alternation with either of the above, in these severe cases, I have seen excellent results from the *Amm. caust.*, prescribed as follows :

℞ Amm. caust., puræ, gtt. x
(**T**) Aquæ distil., - - ℥ vj
M ft. sol. S 10 drops every 30 minutes for six doses; every hour for six doses, and then every two hours.

When the recovery is unusually slow, and typhoid symptoms set in, besides the ordinary medicines that are well known to all practitioners, the following is the most efficacious :

℞ Baptisæ, tinct., gtt. xxx
(**U**) Aquæ font, - - ℥ iv
S a tablespoonful every two hours.

With reference to the preparations of Iron and Bromine, we would here remark, Auburn says that he cured thirty-five cases of this disease out of thirty-nine, with Perchloride of Iron, giving ʒij of a weak solution every five minutes during the day, and every fifteen minutes during the night. The sole food allowed, was an equal quantity of cold milk given after each dose. Crichton says he had equal success with *tr. mur. Ferri*, four to eight drops every two or three hours, together with a local application of a mixture of *tr. mur. Ferri*, and *acid Mur.* dil. Of forty cases, he lost nine*. This is most extraordinary success; but what appears particularly in the case of Auburn to be the nervic *iron* treatment.

Hulte, Rames, and Pluhe,† found, after a long application of *Brom-kali*, coryza; the eyes full of tears; injection of the conjunctiva, with increased sensibility to light. "In larger doses, ʒj pro. dil., it produces intoxication, without any agitation; great malaise; vanishing of strength; decrease of the powers of vision and hearing; loss of all sexual pleasure; insensibility of the skin—even stitches were not felt; fauces and pharynx losing every reflex motion. Usually we give, as soon as we perceive the exudation, the *Brom.* in the following formula:

℞	Brom. o. j., - -	gtt. xij
	Aquæ, distil., -	℥ vij

M. D. S every hour or two a tablespoonful.

The remedy has to be kept from all light, and the first dilution must be always freshly prepared, to be sure to be effectual." The local application is also recommended in the following:

---

* N. A. Journal of Homœopathy, No. XLII, p. 317.

† Dr. L. Lilienthal's Translation from Hirschel's Klinik, N. A. Journal of Homœopathy, No. XLV, p. 114.

℞ Brom· o. j., - - gtt. xx
Glycerini, - - ℥ j

Into this preparation, a camel's hair pencil is dipped, and the substance applied to the affected parts. With this treatment other medicines may be alternated—for instance, *Arsen.*, *China*, *Chinicum* and *Phosphorus*, are the necessary remedies to stay the collapse; also the arsenites of Bromine and Quinine. This is excellent treatment, and will often prove of good service.

The following intercurrent treatment is useful when there is the slightest appearance of cough, viz.—the inhalation of the *vapor of Iodine*, and that medicine of the second dilution, in water, every two hours. The inhalation is conducted as follows: A small tea-pot is filled with boiling water, and a tea-spoonful of pure *tincture of Iodine* poured therein; the patient takes the spout of the vessel in the mouth, and the head being covered with a towel, a few inspirations are made. This method is resorted to when there is no inhaling glass convenient, and it will be found to answer the purpose exceedingly well. The inhalation may be repeated three times during the day. There can be no doubt of the efficacy of this method of treatment, viz: *Iodine*, internally and topically by inhalation, in severe diphtheritis, even after the cough has *commenced;* I have witnessed its efficacy several times, and would have others test it in similar cases.

The following is the published experience of many eminent professional gentlemen of our school—all appearing; however, to agree—with a single exception, which will be alluded to hereafter —that *Aconite*, *Belladonna*, *Arsenicum*, *Iodine*, *Bromine*, the preparations of *Mercury* and of *Potash*, possess a certain degree of influence over the disorder.

Mr. Gelston mentions *Arum Maculatum*, *Aconite*, *Clematis*, *Croton tig.*, *Euphorbium*, *Ranunculus*, *Staphysagria*, *Colchicum*, *Drosera* and *Rhus*, as medicines adapted to Diphtheria; but writes, "of these, I have had experience chiefly with *Aconite;* my observation, however limited, disposes me to place great reliance on its efficacy."*

Mr. Curie recommends *Bryonia* as a specific, having lost but one out of twenty-five cases.

On none of these, with the exception of *Croton tig.*, so far as my own experience goes, should reliance be placed in severe cases.

Dr. J. P. Dake, of Pittsburgh,† prescribes, at the outset, *Belladonna* and *Capsicum* in alternation, every two hours; if the disease advance, the *iodide* of *Mercury* in alternation—one day with *Bella.*, the next with *Capsicum*—giving one dose of the mercurial to two of the other remedies, the interval being two hours between the doses. If the exudation appears, he uses *Nitric acid*, 1st, in four tablespoonsful of water, in alternation with *Bella.* and *Capsicum*, as above noted. In the aphthous form, *Borax*, 2d, with either *Bella.*, *Capsicum* or *Nitric acid;* and in the later stages, *Bromine* and *Bella.* He also states, that he has used, with gratifying results,

* British Journal of Homœopathy, Vol. LXXVII, p. 418.

† North American Journal of Homœopathy, Vol. X, p. 429.

Ammonium causticum, by nasal inhalation, but has not found benefit from the internal administration of the drug.

Dr. Walter Williamson, of Philadelphia, uses, with great success, *Croton tig.*, *Cantharides* and *Rhus tox.*, and thus writes:* "The result of the adoption in my practice, of *Croton*, *Canth.* and *Rhus*, as the principal remedies in the treatment of the throat symptoms in Diphtheria, has been to *diminish the mortality one-half.* A careful study of the pathogeneses of these drugs, and a full consideration of their well-known spheres of action in the treatment of other diseases, would lead one to anticipate important results in the treatment of Diphtheria, and after repeated trials I have found the anticipation to be fully justified."

Dr. Preston† speaks very highly of the *Biniodide of Mercury;* he says it is the best combination of iodine for true Diphtheria, and that he has, thus far, met "with no case that did not promptly and evidently yield to the biniodide ; and, in our hands, it has proved *the specific* for the present epidemic without the use of gargles, or any kind of topical application, external or internal."

Dr. Colton‡, of Chicago, in a well written article, has given very many medicines and the indications for their use, but more particularly describes the general symptoms that may be present in the different forms of the affection.

---

* North American Journal of Homœopathy, Vol. XI. p. 170.

† United States Journal of Homœopathy, Vol. I, p. 242.

‡ Op. Cit., p. 235.

The *Phytolacca Decandria* has been very highly spoken of in Diphtheria. The following are the pathogenetic effects of the drug as reported by Dr. Wm. H. Burt:*

"Constant dull frontal headache, aggravated by motion. Drawing sensation above the root of the nose. Pressure in the eyes; dull aching pains in the eyes. Loss of taste. Tongue is very rough, with blisters on the sides that smart severely. Pressing pain in the right side of the throat. Sore throat, with great roughness in the pharynx. Constant inclination to swallow, which produces severe pains in the root of the tongue and fauces. Violent inflammation of the soft palate and tonsils; the left tonsil is swollen as large again as the right. Thick white and yellow mucus about the fauces. Violent inflammation of the œsophagus down to the stomach. Food produces severe pain the whole length of the œsophagus; feeling as if something had lodged in the œsophagus. Profuse hemorrhage from the nose. Loss of appetite. Urine strongly albuminous. Bowels either constipated or loose. Violent aching of the back, and limbs very weak and faint."

Dr. Burt then reports several cases successfully treated by this medicine.

Dr. Potter, also, regards it as of the greatest possible service in the treatment of the most malignant cases†; and my friend, Dr. Hale,‡ records the

---

* American Homœopathic Observer, No. III, p. 35. Also, the Medical Investigator, Vol. I, p. 30.

† Western Homœopathic Observer. No. VII, p. 60.

‡ New Provings, p. 317.

experience of Drs. Geo. F. Foster, G. C. Brown, C. W. Boyce and Stearns, all testifying to the great applicability of the *Poke* in this disease.

Dr. Couch,* of Fredonia, New York, at the semi-annual meeting of the Homœopathic Medical Society of that State, read a paper on the importance of *Guaiacum officinale*, as a remedy in Diphtheria: and in a letter from Dr. Kenyon, of Buffalo, I am informed that Dr. Beers has been very successful in the treatment of the disease by this medicine alone. The directions for its use, are, to mix half a drachm of the mother tincture with a tumbler half full of sweet milk, and of this mixture to give a dessert spoonful every one, two or three hours, in accordance with the violence of the attack.

Dr. Davies,† in his article, "What is Diphtheria," has found service, in the cases he relates, from *Arsenicum*, *Kali-chlor.*, locally. The *iod. Merc.*, *Nit. acid* and *Gelseminum.*

Dr. Ozanne‡ recommends *Bromine*, and the *bromide of Potassium.*

Dr. Black,§ the *iod. Merc.*, *Muriatic* and *Sulphuric acids*, with *Cantharides.*

Dr. Kidd,|| *Iodine*, particularly, though combined in some instances with other medicines.

---

* American Homœopathic Observer et N. A. Journal of Homœopathy, Vol. XIII, p. 102.

† Op. Cit., No. XLI, p. 100.

‡ Monthly Homœopathic Review, May and June, 1857, p. 448.

§ British Journal of Homœopathy, Vol. XVII, p. 619.

|| British Journal of Homœopathy, Vol. XVII, p. 218.

Dr. Smith* has used successfully, *Ars.*, *Iod.*, *Kali-chlor*, *Nit. ac.*, and *Am. caust.*

Dr. J. V. Hobson, of Richmond, Va., in a paper entitled, "Observations on Diphtheria,"† makes three varieties of diseases, viz :

1st. Croup, or laryngo-tracheitis diphtherica ;

2d. Thrush, including apthæ and stomatitis diphtherica ;

3d. Diphtheria, characterized by adynamia, and which, in reference to the blood change, might be called hæmitis diphtherica, or toxæmia diphtherica (albuminosa?), speaks as follows, in reference to the treatment: "Hartmann recommends *Baryta carbonica* and *Cantharides*. I have never tried them, feeling assured that the disease, as it exists in this country, would not yield to them. They will be found useful, however, for some of the sequelæ."

He then remarks that the chief reliance must be placed on those medicines which have already been mentioned ; and, according to his experience, *Belladonna* corresponds to the internal symptoms of cerebral congestion, sore mouth, &c., while *Causticum* should be recommended where there is deficient systematic reaction.

He has tried, also, with success, *Kali-bich.* and *Merc. prot.*, in alternation. The first triturations being most satisfactory in the cases in which the medicines were exhibited.

---

* British Journal of Homœopathy, Vol. XVIII, p. 100.

† United States Journal of Homœopathy, Vol. I, p. 248.

Dr. Morgan* published ten successfully treated cases, the medicines being *Bell.*, *Merc.*, *Merc. jod.*

Dr. Snelling† places much confidence in *Bromine*, *acid Mur.*, and *Kali-chlor.*

Dr. Raymond has recommended *Kali-bich.*, *Merc. iod.*, *Arsen.*, and *Am. carb.*

But the most extraordinary treatment of Diphtheria is that of Drs. Hering, Lippe, and Reichelm, of Philadelphia, as reported by the former to the American Institute of Homœopathy, and handed down to posterity in the published records of that Society. The medicines were *Belladonna*, then *Bryonia* and *Antimonium crudum*—the latter, it is alleged, suited the *genus epidemicus* exceedingly well.

If the throat presented great sensibility to touch, without swelling, *Lachesis* was administered. If the diptheritic patients had *dark dair* and *black eyes*, iodine was exhibited—and bromine cured the *blue-eyed* and *blond haired* sufferers. Dr. Hering then says, that no other medicine seemed to him indicated, and, least of all, the *iodide of Mercury.* But there is yet the most important point to be considered. "The *lowest* potency used was the 200 of *Jenichin*, generally, however, the higher; and every single dose of medicine, "even in the worst cases," was allowed to ACT twenty-four hours before any change was made.

Dr. Lippe has had "about a like number of cases," and with similar success, has prescribed

* Monthly Homœopathic Review, Vol. V.

† Pamphlet on Diphtheria, and article in N. A. Journal of Homœopathy.

"nearly the same medicines, in the same potencies."

Dr. Reichelm has had "about eighty cases, has given the 30 potencies, and lost none."

We would beg the reader to contemplate seriously the nature of the disorder which we have been endeavoring to portray, and then to examine his materia medica for the recorded symptoms of the medicines that have been so highly lauded by Dr. Hering, and, if afterward, he desire to exhibit potencies of these medicines, so highly attenuated as the 200 or the 2,000; in the name of common humanity, to record the symptoms of the disease, and the result of the treatment in each individual case, for the benefit of those who yet have not discovered in the Homœopathic Materia Medica, a true specific medicine for the malignant forms of Diphtheria.

For further information on the treatment of the disease, as conducted by the homœopathists of France, the reader is referred to "a report of the proceedings of the Meeting Societe Medicale Homœopathique de France, held January 16th 1860," translated for the British Journal of Homœopathy for October 1st, 1860; and also, for a continuation of the discussion, to a very able paper on the subject, that appeared in the same excellent quarterly for July 1st, 1861.

Some Allœopathic writers have devised a means of—

Prophylaxis of Diphtheria.—M. Loiseau has had twenty years' experience in *tannaging* the throat for the prevention of diphtheritic accidents and croup, and states that his treatment has been very successful. When Diphtheria is epidemic, all adults, on feeling the slightest *mal de gorge*, should immediately gargle with an aqueous solution of tannin every fifteen minutes, occasionally swallowing some drops, in order that every part of the throat may be submitted to the agent's action. If, after twenty-four hours of this simple medication, no amelioration is perceptible, an alcoholic solution of the same substance may be used. The trouble not yet receding, add to the above six or eight grammes of tannin, one or two grammes of chlorforom, and eight grammes of alcohol. If this fails, have recourse to the etherial solution of tannin. In treating a child not old enough to gargle, make it drink very small quantities of one of the above solutions, and at the same time blow some powdered tannin into its throat. The strength of the etherial and alcoholic solutions must, of course be in keeping with the age and susceptibilities of the patient.*

SECTION IV.

Diet.

The diet of a patient affected with diphtheritis is by no means an unimportant point, and one which is too much overlooked by our particular school. Diphtheria, we believe, to be essentially an albu-

* Vide American Medical Times, March 15, 1862.

minous condition of the blood, and, therefore, it is better to select those articles of diet which are known to contain the least of that substance.

1. Isinglass contains from	8 to 13	per cent.	of albumen.
2. Sweet bread contains	14.00	"	"
3. White of egg "	15.5	"	"
4. Yolk " "	17.47	"	"
5. Ox liver "	20.19	"	"
6. Caviare "	31.00	"	"

It is well known that these articles are frequently brought to the sick room, and they must be rejected as decidedly objectionable, while either of the following should be given:

Flesh of	beef	contains	of albumen	2.2 per cent.
"	venison	"	"	2.3 "
"	mutton	"	"	2.6 "
"	veal	"	"	2.6 to 3.2 per cent.
"	chicken	"	"	3.0 per cent.
"	fish	"	"	4.4 to 5.2 per cent.
"	pigeon	"	"	4.5 per cent.

The better method is to make an essence of beef, mutton, venison, or chicken, and give it in spoonful doses as frequently as every hour. At the same time, wine-whey may be allowed frequently, or other stimulant; in some instances, brandy and water is necessary. The system is overloaded by a poison in the blood; the disease is rapid in its course, and as much nutrition as possible should be allowed to the patient. By this I do not wish it to be understood that food and drink should be crammed into the stomach at all times, but I do mean, that if there be a slight appetite, or if the patient can be persuaded to take such nourishment as will assist nature and the medicine to support the constitution, and throw off the disease, that it is the duty of every conscientious physician to do every thing in his power to accomplish such an end. I know that by such remarks I am not expressing the views of very many homœopathists, but I am guided only by my own experience in these matters; and I am convinced that life has, perhaps, been saved, and further development of membrane prevented, by the proper selection of nutritious and stimulating diet in Diphtheria.

In some instances, if the disease appear to be stationary, neither advancing nor receding, injections of beef tea and arrow root may be of signal service; they do no harm, and may, perhaps, be productive of much benefit.

CHAPTER VIII.—SURGICAL OPERATIONS.

In the treatment of Diphtheria, surgical interference is, in the majority of instances, of doubtful utility; the use of instruments causes additional pain, and, in many cases, is absolutely uncalled for, and, in other instances, death is hastened by the blundering surgeon, who, disregarding the true nature of the disorder, seeks, by mechanical means, to arrest a local disease, while the patient is succumbing to a constitutional poison; yet there have been instances in which life has been prolonged, and death averted by the skillful use of the knife; and, although favorable terminations, after surgical operations, in Diphtheria, are not very numerous, yet, in so malignant a disease, it becomes the duty of the physician to render his patient the benefit of all the known means of relief, and to exercise the discrimination in every case that would either justify the attempt to save life by operative procedure, or to forbid, positively, any such hazardous undertaking.

Let us, therefore, examine the matter carefully, and view it in varied lights, before either positively contemning, or extravagantly praising, the efforts made by the surgeon in his attempts to combat the disease.

The manner of death, in Diphtheria, is different in different patients. In the one instance, the exudation may form rapidly upon the tonsils, uvula and rima-glottidis, and threaten suffocation by its presence, while the "vocal box" and the trachea may not be the least affected: in such a case as this, the question arises, could not laryngotomy or tracheotomy be performed upon a patient of good constitution and of previous robust health? The physician cannot be expected to say positively that the respiratory organs will be affected; and, when the fact is remembered, that a majority of cases of pharyngeal Diphtheria recover, the propriety of operating would certainly become a question of the greatest importance: but, on the other hand, death frequently results from general zymosis and from perfect anæmia; the breathing is easier, deglutition perfect, and, in such an instance, it were ruthless brutality to inflict the pain of a surgical operation. No surgeon, in his senses, could resort to, nay, even think, of such a proceeding. Or, again, death may take place from suffocation, engendered by the presence of the membrane within the larynx and trachea ; and here also I believe that the use of the knife is perfectly uncalled for—most certainly when the *trachea* is involved.

The surgical operations which have been recommended are—ablation of the tonsils, laryngotomy, tracheotomy, and tubage of the glottis—of these we now propose to speak.

SECTION I.

Ablation of the Tonsils.

I have known excision of the tonsils, in one or two instances, be productive of great benefit to the patient—allowing much more facility of respiration, and removing a considerable portion of false membrane. In both cases, where the operation was performed, the children recovered, and in the instance which has already been detailed in a former chapter of this work, it will be perceived that great temporary benefit resulted. It would be very ridiculous to assert that excision of the tonsils is a *remedy* for Diphtheria ; it can only be resorted to as a palliative means to arrest suffocation for the time, *and should only be employed when such suffocation is evidently about to produce asphyxia and death.*

M. Bouchut states*—

* United States Journal of Homœopathy, Vol. I.

1st. That amputation of the tonsils is an excellent prevention of croup.

2d. That the ablation of the tonsils in diphtheric angina, is absolutely necessary when these glands are swollen enough to obstruct the hæmatosis, and when the respiratory vesicular murmur, extremely feeble, can scarcely be heard.

3d. That there is no reason to fear the reproduction of false membranes on the wound of the tonsils, and that the nature of the disease does not counter-indicate the operation.

4. That this amputation occasions no serious hemorrhage, the slight local bleeding being rather advantageous.

5th. That the wounded tonsils heal in this case like a simple wound, and after only a few days of suppuration.

6. That in order to succeed, this means ought only to be employed in cases where the diphtheric angina exists alone, and without complication with false membranes of the larynx.

The methods of performing the operation are so well known and so simple, that it is scarcely necessary to allude to them here. I would only remark, that, in many cases, the ordinary instrument of Fanhestock is too small at its circular extremity to admit the enlarged gland within it; and that an ordinary tenaculum and scissors, or bistoury, have, with me, proved preferable. If the child is young, and the instrument be sufficiently large, it may be used with advantage.

At best, however, amputation of the tonsils can

only be had recourse to in a few instances, and must be regarded as a palliative means. The true secret in the treatment, of course, being the internal medication.

SECTION II.

Tracheotomy.

The results after the operation for tracheotomy in croup, are not very satisfactory, and in Diphtheria, they are, as far as my own observation, reading and experience extends, still less so. I can call to mind but six cases in which the operation has been performed in Diphtheria, one of which is said to have proved successful. One of these cases occurred in my own practice, the operation being performed at the very urgent solicitation of the friends and relatives of the patient.

Cases, however, have occurred, in which the post-mortem examinations revealed no extension of the membranous deposit within the trachea, wherein perhaps tracheotomy may have been advisable.

In those autopsies which are published in the chapter on pathology, the trachea was not found involved, but the general condition of the patient forbade any attempt at surgical performance.

In all such cases, however, the judgment of the physician must be carefully exercised, and the true character of the disease, and the successes and failures of the operation stated fully to the patient, or to his friends, before the knife is resorted to.

On this point, Greenhow writes:* "Upon this subject, I have no personal experience, but the operation in this country has been almost always unsuccessful. On the other hand, I have had the opportunity, in two instances, of observing, in *post-mortem* examinations, that the false membrane extended a very short distance down the trachea, and in one of these, death appeared to have been caused by the partially separated membrane acting as an obstruction to the admission of air. Perhaps, in this instance, the performance of tracheotomy might have saved the patient; and when the case appears to be otherwise hopeless, it would probably be right to give the patient the chance afforded by the operation, provided there should be no evidence of the extension of the disease to the bronchial tubes, or of the existence of pneumonia, either of which would manifestly contra-indicate the performance of an operation, which must, under such circumstances, prove unavailing." It will appear from this, that, in the opinion of Greenhow, tracheotomy is not considered of much import. On the other hand, Dr. Slade† remarks: "Without going into a history of tracheotomy, or a recapitulation of the arguments on the one side or the other, we most unhesitatingly say, that, under the circumstances above mentioned, this operation is a resource which we are in duty bound to employ for the safety of our patients, and in view of what experience teaches us, is otherwise certain death.

* Diphtheria, p. 150.

† Diphtheria; its nature and treatment, p. 70.

It is not by so doing that we increase his chances for life solely, but in the case of an unfavorable termination, we render his last moments less distressing."

Speaking on the subject of tracheotomy, Dr. A. L. Voss,* at a stated meeting of the New York Academy of Medicine, held March 28th, 1862, says: "It is worthy of remark, that I have not yet heard of a successful operation in New York during the year 1859, famous for Diphtheria."

Here might follow any number of statistics of the operation, which are very numerous, and are recorded in most works upon the diseases of children, in the text books upon Surgery, Medical Dictionaries, &c. Many of these are not of recent date, and can be found by any practitioner who takes interest sufficient in the subject to make the necessary investigations.

SECTION III.

Tubing the Larynx.

This proceeding has been mentioned, and even recommended, as a cure for Diphtheria; but as the cases which have been subjected to the operation were not at all successful, and none of them were those of true Diphtheria, it appears that all that can be said of the procedure, is merely to reject it as inefficient.

---

* American Medical Times, May 10th, 1862, p. 265.

The operation consists in inserting into the larynx metallic tubes, which may be retained for a longer or shorter time, according to the circumstances of the case. M. Bouchut claims the honor of having introduced the operation, or, rather, of having modified an old idea, with reference to the tolerance of the larynx to foreign substances properly inserted; but, from all that I can read upon the subject—and I confess that though I have examined several recent works, and even "Bouchut's Diseases of Children," wherein I expected to find some mention of the "tubage"—I have been mostly disappointed. The following extract, however, will suffice:

"Chaussier employed for laryngeal insufflations a curved canula, flattened at the end, with two eyes, wide above and narrowing below. Such is the instrument recently employed by Dr. Loiseau in order to avoid tracheotomy. This means had been used by Dieffenbach at the Charity Hospital of Berlin, in 1839, and Dr. Bouchut, of St. Eugenie, at Paris, has only modified it in his famous 'tubage of the glottis.' The curved sounds employed have rings to protect the finger or dilators inserted between the teeth. They are not difficult of introduction, and do not hinder the play of the epiglottis, nor of the arytenoidean cartilages; the inferior *chordæ vocales* come between the two swellings of the canula, consequently above the lower one, corresponding to the internal face of the cricoid cartilage. By the application of such an instrument, M. Bouchut and others have succeeded in averting imminent asphyxia; cyanosis, suffocation and anæsthesia have ceased, and the canula remained in the glottis thirty-six hours, without embarrassing its functions. The child speaks more clearly than before the insertion of the tube; can drink without the liquids falling into the air-passages, and can cough up false membranes through the canula, so that it seems to fulfill all mechanical indications."

These surgical performances are thus briefly alluded to, in order that each physician may discover, if he deem it necessary to resort to surgical means in the treatment of any particular case of Diphtheria, that a work which proposes to be a treatise on the same, will not be found entirely devoid of information on the subjects in question.